A TREKKER'S HANDBOOK

D0532881

Alpine, Layla Spire, Pakistan

A TREKKER'S HANDBOOK

by

TOM GILCHRIST

CICERONE PRESS
MILNTHORPE, CUMBRIA

A TREKKER'S HANDBOOK

© Tom Gilchrist 1996
ISBN 1 85284 205 9
A catalogue record for this book is available from the British Library

This book is for Douglas

ACKNOWLEDGEMENTS

I would like to thank the following: my Mum and Dad, for buying me my first pair of boots and pointing me in the right direction. Julie, for not letting me give up on this, for hours of typing, proof reading and editing, but most of all for her company and patience. John MacP for his endless encouragement, enthusiasm, proof reading and the use of his PowerBook! Dr Liz Merry, for checking the medical sections so thoroughly at such short notice, and to the Dept. of Health for all their help. Mossy and the Nevis Rangers for their computer skills, time and hardware. John E., Claire, my Dad and Mark for sharing their stories with me and allowing them to be printed. And thanks to Vic Saunders for his kind words. Tim, Glen and Kit for so much information and help.

Thanks to everyone at the Lochaber Centre for being so tolerant when I was there in body but not totally in mind. To Lyn, Sue, Ali and Orna. Yes! I'm still here! To Paul, Mark M., Dave W., Dave L., Martin, Graham and Juliet. Just to let you know that you have all left your mark. And finally, to all the friends I have made whilst trekking - too many by far to mention. Thank you for giving me your riches!

Front Cover : Pokaldy, Nepal

CONTENTS

FOREWORD

I like hearing voices. I don't mean *those* sort of voices. I mean writing. It has to be audible to hold my interest. I like dialogue that is so acute you can tell the accent of the speaker. I like to hear the author write as freely as he or she speaks. I like to hear that idiolect that tells you who you are listening to, when really all you are doing is reading. And so, I like this book. Tom Gilchrist has his own way of speaking and that is the way he writes. If you never met Tom before reading this, you'd recognise him from his voice. It leaps out of the pages at you. And what this voice tells you about Trekland, gentle reader, is the result of half a lifetime knocking around the Himalaya, Karakoram and Hindu Kush. This book is not a guide, it doesn't do the trek for you as so many guides do. No. This book will equip you to carry out your own adventures. Gilchrist assumes you are reasonably intelligent, and curious about the world you live in. Well, I don't suppose you would be reading this if you were not. This book is simply advice from one observant and intelligent visitor to another. So, my advice to you is, listen to this book and enjoy. You do like hearing voices, don't you? Of course you do.

Victor Saunders, 1995

Introduction

"The real purpose of climbing, and of any other sport, should be to transmute it into a way of living, however temporary, in an environment which appeals to the individual....

There are few treasures of more lasting worth than the experiences of a way of life that is in itself wholly satisfying. Such, after all, are the only possessions of which no fate, no cosmic catastrophe can deprive us; nothing can alter the fact if for one moment in eternity we have really lived." Eric Shipton

"They walked on, thinking of this and that..."

Winnie the Pooh *(A.A. Milne)*

This book is about people and places. It is about the relationships between man and his environment, and the relationships between people of different cultures. Its issues concern people within a group, and people within themselves. It is these issues, resolved, ignored, abused or unabated that create, to whatever degree, quality within any trek. This book is about Karma, inner peace, strength and knowledge, the keys to the locks forged from ignorance, preconceived ideas, fear and arrogance. There is also quite a lot about creepy crawlies and unsavoury medical complaints. Let us seek enlightenment through hard facts. Knowledge from the experiences of others. Inner peace from the comfort created by careful preparation and consideration for others and for the land. Zen and the art of Trekking, it's cosmic, Man.

This book is not intended to be a 'survival' guide, but more a comfort guide. Survival implies that there has been a very close shave and we don't want that. I want you to give the grim Reaper a very wide berth indeed, and I would like this book to help others do the same. This is the trekkers' equivalent to cloves of garlic and wooden stakes. Comfort is where it's at. Those with a Tilmanesque bent might see discomfort as being the price of adventure. I view it as an unsavoury and avoidable by-product that absorbs time that is better spent in appreciating what is going on around one. Being comfortable should not distract from the excitement of the situation.

Uncomfortable people create an atmosphere of discomfort around them. Fine if you're only passing. Suppose you have to spend weeks with them though? Suppose that person is you? Gloom, despair and a poor quality adventure. Think of all the people involved in a trek: trekkers, leaders, Sirdars, cooks, porters and villagers. It wouldn't do to have uncomfortable (unhappy) people in such a micro society. Every trek should be viewed as a one off, unique experience. An opportunity to discover the delights of a new (or your own) land, different cultures, foods, climates. A once-in-a-lifetime chance to push yourself mentally and physically, to sit and contemplate, to view the landscape, make new friends and consider the other man's lot. Recharge the batteries.

So it really should be done properly.

'Trek' was a fairly everyday word in Holland until the Boers took it across the Transvaal and put a bit of meat on its bones. To trek meant more than to walk; to them it was synonymous with hardship and endeavour - those treks were epic journeys of exploration and discovery with freedom the motive and personal gain the reward. They may have been driven by need and ambition but they certainly weren't the first to do so. Since before *Homo sapiens* knew that's what they were, they were off into the next valley heading for the horizon, hunting, trading, and paying homage to their gods.

As the societies developed so did the professional trader. And as he developed so did his trade routes. Using trade, cultural enlightenment, religion and the Empire as faint excuses, others travelled for sheer adventure. From Marco Polo through the Jesuits to the exploits of the Victorians, roads and paths were trodden through valleys, over passes, across plains and around mountains basically for the joy of it. By the turn of this century, the pretence was almost over and the rich embarked on the first treks, using the further flung ends of the Empire as spring-boards into the world's remotest places. People like the deliciously eccentric Bullock-Workmans and later the amazing Robert and Katherine Barrett made incredible journeys, initially along well established routes, then on the lesser known routes progressing to little known tracks and local paths, finally succumbing to crossing unknown country to forge links between ancient trade and pilgrimage routes. Those who depend on the soil for survival tend to give mountains a wide berth and it's no surprise therefore that even up to the early 1930s very little was known of the Great Ranges of the world. Goatherds and pilgrims wandered the mountains but it wasn't until the arrival of the mountaineers that their inner sanctums were fully explored. Often working on the reports and sightings of early trekkers, these mountaineers forged routes into some of the wildest, most spectacular scenery it is possible to imagine.

Names like Shipton, Tilman and Herzog come readily to mind, but every country has its mountaineering heroes. In the days before aerial reconnaissance and hyper-efficient communications, mountaineering expeditions were unavoidably huge affairs and more often than not necessitated the need for exploratory expeditions simply to find a route into the mountains. Again using established routes as starting points, these expeditions probed and pushed their way into the heart of the peaks and to the bases of mountains that are now household names: Annapurna, K2, Nandi Devi and Mount Everest itself. On one of these expeditions to Annapurna in 1950 was one Colonel Jimmy Roberts, who is reckoned to be the father of trekking as we know and love it today. In 1965 he founded 'Mountain Travel' in Kathmandu, Nepal, a country in which he had served for many years. Using his local knowledge and hard earned connections he took people into the heart of the Himalaya, previously only visited by mountaineering expeditions and a few adventurous individuals, on a commercial basis. Whilst these treks may have been tough on the legs and lungs, Col Roberts initiated the luxurious camp standards which have now become synonymous with Nepal. Col Roberts knew about comfort... Almost immediately there were rival agencies established, but it was the international overland travel companies who really established trekking as a travel market commodity.

By the mid 1970s overland travel was losing its appeal. Borders had toughened due to the usual wars and diplomatic bickering and there was a breed of more adventurous, but affluent, clients looking around the market place. Society had changed in that there was a steady rise in childless professionals with more disposable income, and an interest in the outdoors that strayed beyond the West. Aiming for their custom, and using their established travel businesses, the Overland Companies moved towards trekking and advertised treks to potential clients in the USA, Europe and Australasia. By the mid 1980s trekking was big business and here to stay. As the companies grew bigger, in size and number, so did their itineraries. Now it is possible to take a commercial trek in any of the continents in the world. Some are a bit expensive, though having said that, where there are commercial rivals there are price wars, and it's never been easier and cheaper in real terms for the individual to travel to destinations that were once the reserve of the rich, the diplomatic elite or the insatiably curious and determined.

This great commercial interest in trekking affects us all. To what degree is up to the individual; the trick is to use it to your advantage, to see through its cons and maximise its pros. Trekking is a sensory massage, an experience that thrills the ears, the eyes and touch. The mind will race, pulling the artist and poet in you to the fore, and relax, leaving home, and its worries, in the cellar of your soul. And if it's only for a few short days or weeks, it will still be worthwhile because the memories of it will be ingrained and linger on.

I've tried to keep the contents of the book as uncomplicated as possible and the information contained within, relevant. Most of the facts are answers to basic queries that my colleagues and myself have been asked about time and

The Lowari Pass, North West Frontier Province, Pakistan

time again., The opinions, I hope, will serve to provoke thought and to ask questions about what, on the surface, is a walking holiday.

I sincerely hope most of the advice and information to follow proves to be superfluous. Despite all the procedures, precautions and routines involved in a good trek, the majority of hours in each day is still spent walking, viewing, thinking, relaxing, laughing, eating, drinking, sunning, reading, writing and any other good "ing" one can think of.

CHAPTER ONE
Choosing a trek and getting there

"You know, Alf, going to the right place, at the right time, with the right people is all that really matters. What one does is purely incidental."
Colin Kirkus to Alf Bridge on the summit of Sgurr Alasdair

JOHN'S STORY
"'Bed Tea Bed Tea!' I emerged from the depth and warmth of my sleeping bag to the familiar Sherpa early morning greeting. Looking at my watch I saw that it was 1am; I had been awakened to complete the final phase of a two week trek and an attempt to climb a 6,000m Himalayan trekking peak. A glance at the thermometer suspended outside the tent showed the reading to be minus 25 degrees centigrade and as I settled back into my sleeping bag only one thought crossed my mind: "What on earth am I doing here?" This feeling was reinforced as a hand appeared through the tent holding a lumpy bowl of porridge - my breakfast!

Camped at over 5,500m any movement takes a supreme amount of effort. With the intense cold I had gone to bed fully clothed but it still took something approaching half an hour before I was able to adjust my mind to the fact that I now had to step outside the tent. As I emerged, it was to see other members of my group already struggling with plastic boots and crampons at this unearthly time of the day. As we all tried to shake off the effects of lack of sleep at altitude very few words were spoken, each person wrapped up in their own world. All around was pitch black with only a reflection of the moon on the snow giving some light. As we trudged off up the slope on what was the final seven hours to the summit, some life came back to my body although it was to be a full two hours before my feet started to feel warmed up. Gradually the splendour of our surroundings and the excitement of the challenge began to overcome the cold and tiredness. I was roped up to and relying on five people to whom I had become closer over the past three weeks than I had to many people over a lifetime. Thrown together on a trek we had lived and walked together, shared experiences both worrying and wonderful. In the remote areas in which we had been living as one with the land, there were no secrets.

As dawn broke we reached a relatively flat ridge giving us views across the Himalaya all around us. In the east there was the huge triangle of Makalu, the

Jeep on a scary bridge, Darkot, Pakistan

fifth-highest mountain in the world flanked by lesser but still spectacular peaks. In the south, the foothills of Nepal were still cloaked in the pre-dawn mist. To the north, the mountains that marked the border with Tibet changed from a cold blue to a golden red, and over in the west the mighty peaks of the Langtangs and the Annapurnas emerged from the gloom. As we walked along the ridge, I was overcome by a sense of freedom and emotion. I was seeing sights that very few people were lucky enough to see and it made all the effort and hardship of the previous few weeks worthwhile. In a remote part of the mountain with only ourselves and our Sherpas for company, surrounded by such peacefulness and beauty, it was hard to imagine anything else that might have been going on in other parts of the world. With such simple pleasures as this, it made a mockery of all those contraptions that we take for granted at home to make life happier and simpler but which, in actual fact, result in the reverse.

"John, it's for you". I was brought back to reality with a call from my colleague. Suddenly I was back in my office surrounded by computer screens and telephones. As always when coming back from a trek, I was finding it hard to readjust to normal everyday life. It has always seemed strange to me that I never seem to have a difficulty adjusting to what are undoubtedly the tougher experiences that one has on trek. It now feels very familiar sitting down for dinner on the first evening in the mess tent eating off cheap metal plates and drinking plenty of sweetened black tea. The experiences that one has on trek are such that it is very difficult to explain them fully to one's family and friends and especially to those who have not experienced it.

I was first drawn to the idea of trekking by many years of walking in the British hills. I have always had a fascination with the Himalaya and in particular with Mount Everest. Having been trekking once, it then became addictive. Trekking holidays take you to countries that have more fascination than mountains alone. Whether it is Nepal, India, Pakistan or possibly one of the former Soviet states, you come into contact with groups of people of both different religion and culture to your own. Once up into the high valleys of the big mountains, very little of the twentieth-century way of life exists. There are no roads or telephones. It is very rare to find either electricity or hot water. Water for drinking must be collected from rivers or streams and boiled. Any food must be carried on one's back.

Many people are mortified at the thought of some of the lack of amenities on trek, but I suspect that if they decided to "take the plunge" they would not find the hardships as great as they had feared.

After returning from a trek I feel both elated and sad. After spending several weeks living and walking in remote mountain areas one builds up an affinity with the surroundings. Having come to feel at ease in such an environment, it is a wrench to be confronted with the twentieth century again. Mind you, a soak in a long, hot bath does help! I would always feel that a part of me had remained in the mountains and would constantly find myself lapsing into daydreams about my experiences, very often several weeks after I had returned.

An important part of the experience is the interaction amongst the remainder of your group. A disparate group of characters is thrown together, living on top of one another in very often difficult conditions for several weeks. A sense of humour and a philosophical attitude are a must. However, the spirit of teamwork and camaraderie that builds up through shared experiences that tend to be extreme whilst trekking produces a strong bond which one tends to miss on returning once the group splits up and goes its own separate ways.

I spent many hours looking at slides and thinking back over the wealth of experiences that one gains whilst trekking, whether it be from the people met along the trail or the satisfaction of completing the challenge of attaining a peak or crossing a high pass. I tend to find that trekking has a calming influence on me and that it takes some time before I am back into the frenetic pace of everyday life. It is the attainment of this peace of mind which is a strong driving force behind the addictive nature of trekking. As with anything that is worthwhile having, it can't be reached without a fair degree of effort, but the rewards are such that it is very difficult to put them into words." *John Eastgate*

CHOOSING A FIRST TREK
Let's go! Yes, but where? The world's your trekking oyster, and deciding where to go, particularly for your first trek, can be a daunting prospect. It's very much a personal thing and rather than recommend a particular place I would like to point out a few things to help you, Dear Reader, make your choice.

Debutantes to the trekking scene have a lot to contend with on that first trek: heat, altitude, prolonged physical and mental exertion, the interaction with other people, choosing and using the right gear, the prospect of illness and how to handle it. And then there's Culture Shock. These days the most popular treks, being in and around the Great Ranges, tend to be based in the Third and Developing Worlds. One aspect of a good trek is the culture and ethos of the host country. I was very lucky when I visited Nepal for the first time to have had a few treks under my belt because, cynical Scot that I am, I was totally unprepared for the effect that the impact of Nepal had on me. Being semi-trekwise allowed me to allot a good proportion of my limited brain to assimilate and absorb the sights, sounds and smells around me without having to worry about whether my boots fitted, or if I was fit enough. It started at the airport when I saw an elephant in the taxi-rank.... One of the joys of

Chitwan taxi rank, Nepal

trekking is that you are right in the midst of what's going on! If you like to live your life at 200mph then go for the big time, but if you're a bit apprehensive then break yourself in a touch gentler by trying something a little closer to home, in a more familiar culture. Not that trekking in Europe or North America is by any means a complete doss; on the contrary, being cooler and lower down it can make for some sustained, tough walking.

Another reason worth considering a closer-to-home first trek is that of cost, in time, money and experience. Regardless of how you arrange your trek in say, Asia, it's going to cost less to get to Europe, and it will be quicker too. It's perfectly feasible also to enjoy a twelve-day trek in a fourteen-day holiday flying from the UK to France or Spain. Two weeks in Asia would be lucky to give you eight or nine days' trekking, more probably six or seven. If trekking is a new experience why waste a three-week holiday and a considerable amount of money only to discover that you get altitude sickness at 1,350m, are prone to sweat rash, are allergic to rice and, strange as it may seem, hate walking? At least you'll have some leave and credit left to allow you to lie on a beach in Spain to moan and recover. A few unprejudiced suggestions, in no particular order, might be:

The Bernese Oberland
Tour of Mont Blanc

The GR.20 in Corsica
The Sierra Nevada in Spain
The Italian Dolomites.

One suggestion with prejudice:

The Haute Route de Pyrenees, one of my favourite places in the whole world, and further afield, and a little more adventurous and different, Morocco, Turkey and the former Soviet Union. If it all works out well and it's obvious that you are Marco Polo reincarnate then you'll be well primed for your next adventure. And if you viewed the Matterhorn wishing it was Everest, don't worry, it'll still be there next year....

SEASON AND WEATHER CONSIDERATIONS

The next consideration is Mother Nature PLC. We are always at her mercy, and despite our technological excellence and advances on trek we are treated by her no better or worse than our cave dwelling ancestors. It is she who provides the spectacle and takes our breath away, filling us with awe, and must therefore be treated with the utmost respect and humility. But she does provide some patterns and phenomena to help us plan our pilgrimages to her most holy of places. This may be basic 'O' level geography, but it's amazing how many people never consider, or choose to ignore, the seasons, the equator and the monsoon. The enclosed tables give a broad overview of what happens with the weather and when, to allow one to plan around it, especially if your holiday dates are not as flexible as you would prefer. For the most part heat is the major influence. Turn up in the Jebel in August and you're in for a hot holiday and no water. Better trying in December and January for a cool(ish) winter break. If this summer/winter thing is all a bit obvious, and you know to reverse the seasons south of the equator, have you considered the monsoon? Just as it's possible to trek in the winter, it's possible to trek through the monsoon, either by avoiding it or by being prepared for it. The Indian/Asian monsoon starts around May in Sri Lanka reaching Nepal about mid June and rolling into the Punjab a month later. By October it's all over bar the shouting until winter arrives at the end of November. This gives two good months post-monsoon and about two pre-monsoon for trekking. Whilst certain areas of the Himalaya above 4,500/5,000m seem exempt from the rain - and it can be as much as a metre per month - they are still prone to the associated turbulent air streams.

Don't view the following table as sacrosanct; it is only a quick overview of what is available and the best times to go there. There is nothing to stop you from wading through the Uganda forests in July or baking your brains in Death Valley during the following month. We are grown-ups and make our own choices.

To a lesser degree East Africa and South America suffer from monsoon but problems tend to be more localised and the general seasons remain the greater problem.

PLACE	BEST TIME TO VISIT	TYPE OF TERRAIN
EUROPE		
France	April-Sep	Cold Desert-Alpine
Spain	April-Sep	Cold Desert-Alpine
Italy	April-Sep	Cold Desert-Alpine
Corsica	April-Sep	Cold Desert-Alpine
Austria	April-Sep	Cold Desert-Alpine
Scandinavia	April-Sep	Cold Desert-Alpine
Greece	April-Sep	Cold Desert-Alpine
Iceland	July-Aug	Cold Desert-Alpine
Eastern Bloc	June-Sep	Cold Desert-Alpine
Switzerland	May-Sep	Cold Desert-Alpine
UK	May-Oct	Cold Desert-Alpine
Turkey	July-Sep	Cold Desert-Alpine
ASIA		
Nepal	Jan-Apr/Oct-Dec	Alpine-Himalayan
Pakistan	May-Sep	Hot Desert-Himalayan
India (N)	July-Aug	Hot Desert-Himalayan
Sikkim		Hot Desert-Himalayan
Bhutan	Apr-May/Sep-Oct	Alpine-Himalayan
Tibet	May-Oct	Cold Desert-Alpine/High Desert
N AFRICA		
Hot Deserts	Nov-May	Hot Desert-Alpine
Mountains	May-Sep	Hot Desert-Alpine
E AFRICA	Dec-Feb/June-Sep	Tropical-Alpine
S AMERICA	Nov-Mar	Cold Desert-Alpine
AUSTRALASIA N	Dec-Feb/July-Nov	
(N S) S	Dec-Mar	Cold Desert-Alpine
ARCTIC	July-Aug	Cold Desert-Alpine
ANTARCTIC	Dec-Jan	Cold Desert-Alpine
N AMERICA		
H. Desert	Oct-Mar	High Desert-Alpine+
Mountains	May-Sep	High Desert-Alpine+

From the outside it is easy to make connections, often false, between the country a trek takes place in, the altitude it takes place at, the type of terrain it crosses, and the degree of difficulty involved in doing so. However there are numerous other factors involved in the equation before one can say a trek is easy, moderate or difficult. Whether you are carrying your own bag, for a start, and the number of Alpine Huts you pass in a day that sell beer, for another. An eight hour walking day can vary so much, as our own countryside can testify, and when you start to examine possible treks outside the UK it should become apparent that regardless of where you want to go, it can be made as easy or as difficult as you want. A slow acclimatising wander in the Khumbu at 14,000ft is going to be much easier than a bog-trotting, river-crossing, rucsack carrying tromp through Iceland. Essentially there are two main considerations: where you want to go, and how hard you want it to be when you get there. I do think that where you want to go should be the prime consideration. If you are at all new to this game, and you really don't have a clue where to go or what to expect and your geography is a bit scant, don't worry. In fact you are in an enviable position, having no preconceived ideas. If you are totally clueless geographically, find out where you live - it helps when you buy a return ticket to know where you are coming back to!

TREKKING ZONES
All manner of countries have all manner of treks and I'll start by giving a rough guide to the trekking environments and their characteristics. Remember, though, that all deserts are not the same despite having a lot in common. (I'll use the same classifications when I talk about equipment later.) I've mentioned deserts so that's where we'll start.

Altitudes quoted in these classifications must be taken with a pinch of salt. The treeline, for instance, tends to get higher nearer to the equator, which can throw some of these descriptions out a bit. Also, don't take altitude too seriously until you have read the section on altitude and acclimatisation.

Deserts (hot)
Hot during the day, cool or even cold at night. Sparsely populated, vegetated and dusty, hard underfoot and, contrary to popular belief, not so flat; it is often hilly or mountainous. Wildlife is highly evolved and adapted to the environment, but does tend to be nocturnal. Flora also highly developed. Despite my description, the desert is anything but bland, and the sharp morning and evening light paints the land with colours richer than a Disney cartoon, its shadows frame sculptures that demonstrate just how feeble an artist man is. It is very brown though. If you're not convinced then read some of Edward Abbey's *Desert Solitaire* or *Beyond the Wall* (an American writer/

philosopher/conservationist with a penchant for the Mid-West USA).

Deserts (cold)
Cold deserts vary immensely, from the Tundra of Alaska and Siberia to the superb cross-country skiing of Antarctica. Geographically these are the cold, wet and windy regions in and around the Arctic and Antarctic circles, supporting dwarf trees and low bushes. Summer is short with long days and the wildlife and flora are varied and hectic during the short summer season. Cold, with much snow and wind during the winter. And, of course, not flat at all.

Sub-alpine 2-3,000m
Rolling hills with green pastures rising to 2-3,000m. Jaggy summits, perhaps the odd patch of permanent snow and the tails of glaciers. Tall, mature, deciduous trees lower down, with evergreens higher up - Deodar cedar, fir, pine, and redwoods. Warm days, cool evenings. Nearer the equator banana trees giving way to groves of bamboo and rhododendron. High summer pastures and summer settlements.

Alpine region 3-4,000m
Rising out of the treeline here, the undergrowth having much in common with the cold deserts. High passes with occasional snow patches. Glaciers to cross. Warm during the day but cold in the shade and when the sun goes down. More rocks and less vegetation with snow on the summits.

Himalayan 4,000m
We're really talking about a high, cold desert, glaciated, with permanent snow on the summits and high passes. Warmish during the day and freezing overnight. Add a few peaks and high technical passes, and you've really reached the upper limit of trekking and are venturing into the world of high altitude mountaineering.

TREKKING GRADES
Having half a clue to the terrain, now think about the difficulty. Commercial operators use their own grading systems, and they should be examined, regardless of whether you are going to travel with them, as they do give a base to work from. Here's a typical brochure description, from the Karakoram Experience trekking company:

EASY - A short easy element of trekking, or easy trekking on most days, and always on good paths, involving altitudes up to 4,000m.

MODERATE - Although some days are fairly strenuous, the majority of trekking is over shorter distances than "easy" grade treks, on paths and tracks and sometimes glaciers. A fairly high level of fitness is needed as high, but straightforward passes are crossed.

DIFFICULT - These treks are more demanding than difficult, involving many days of strenuous walking over difficult terrain including glaciers. A high level of stamina and fitness is required as these treks offer a sustained physical challenge.

VERY DIFFICULT - This grade is reserved for the most difficult treks, involving difficult pass crossings using ropes and mountaineering techniques, often in isolated areas with prolonged periods between 5,000 and 6,000m.

If there is any doubt in your mind at all then go for an easy trek. If it is too easy then all that will happen is that you will catch up on your sleep, read a lot, take many photos, write a book, lots of postcards, contemplate your navel and learn to speak Inuit, or whatever. It'll be like...a holiday.

TREKKING WITH CHILDREN

And why not? Youngsters are more resilient than most people give them credit for and have a natural curiosity and openness that often adds new perspective to the surroundings on trek. As ambassadors, children are unsurpassed and are capable of opening some unique doors, denied to most of us. Even the most cynical locals have a soft spot for little ones and respect for their accompanying adults, a situation that will not change for a long, long time to come. Most children have not learned to be prejudiced and will gleefully play, through all sorts of barriers, with other children, locals, the service crew and other trekkers, once, of course, the initial awe of being on trek and being in Trekland has eased a bit.

No matter how informed the child, the decision to go trekking lies with the adult. The adult must ensure that the trek is designed to suit them, not vice versa. Whilst we adults may revel in a hard day with a spectacular sunset as a finale, junior may simply get grumpy and bored. Be prepared for short days and Lego bricks and stories at bedtime. Has anyone met a small child who didn't enjoy camping? Tents bring the world down to a wendy-house scale and missing out on the nightly bath is not a common subject of conversation, if at all. Watch that stove though...

The down side is the child's intolerance to health hazards. A tendency to play in the dirt, put fingers in mouths and a universal inability to take on board any more than 50 per cent of any healthy (boring) advice does leave one's heirs more susceptible to illness than us sensible (boring) adults. Also whilst children may be clever, they usually don't have as much common sense as we do, little as that is, and will shed clothes in the sun, play near dangerous streams, pick up scorpions to show you. Healthwise, youngsters are not as articulate in describing the symptoms of illness, and become frightened easier and are harder to placate. Be warned.

Children are more prone to altitude sickness than adults, and because of this the rate of ascent must be halved and the number of rest days doubled (see On Trek Health). But children do acclimatise, as the growing population in many mountain villages testifies.

Yes, take children on trek, but be prepared to plan the whole trip round them, hire a nappy/toybox/tired baby porter and keep a special eye out for them when it's cold, hot, high or unhealthy.

Should you see eye to eye with WC Fields ("Love children, but I couldn't eat a whole one") or you are a teacher, then an under 16 is probably the last person you want to share your holiday with. If you've signed up for a commercial trip check with the operators that there will be no children on your trek. Conversely, if you have signed up with your fledgling, check that it's okay with everyone else. Having said all that, I've only ever heard of two under 16s going on a commercially organised trek, so it is a very rare occurrence. Some companies do have lower age limits.

WHAT KIND OF TREKKING GROUP?
The size and style of your trekking group will obviously dictate the amount of preparation necessary, and here's a look at the most popular ways of trekking going on just now. Even as we read.

Solo
Travelling solo gives you all the decisions to make, whether enjoyable or not, for better or for worse. Of course that responsibility also equates to freedom, and trekking alone need not be lonely if the trek takes place in a populated region, or is one of the world's popular treks. Schedules can be altered without consultation and meals cooked properly and the menu tailored to suit. Early starts and long lies are an everyday option, as are rest days, long days and late nights. It is easier to become absorbed into local life and cultures and there are very few rendezvous to rendezvous at. But support is handy sometimes, especially if one becomes ill, the ground is dangerous or there is a load to share. Solo travellers are more susceptible to the nasty side of life too - attacks and worse.

Small group
Trekking with a small group of friends, with perhaps a porter and/or a cook to ease the domestic chores a bit, has most of the good points of being alone with a lot of security and support thrown in. Organisation-wise, preparation

has to be tighter and whilst one person can be squeezed onto a flight, or into a tea-house, two, three, four or five aren't going to quite get away with it. But the intimacy of a family size group is very uplifting if you enjoy sharing discovery with others.

On a commercial trip small group dynamics can make or break the trek depending on how people mix and get on. Part of the enjoyment can be getting to know the others, listening to their stories, sharing their experiences, beating them at chess and so on. But if you don't like most, or all, of the others, then you're stuck in an unpleasant situation.

Large group
We are talking about ten to fifteen trekkers here plus the accompanying support crew. The advantages of being part of a large group? Well, if it is a privately organised party, doing what you like doing best, with the people you like most. Organisation and responsibility are shared, with a degree of concern and commitment not always found in a commercially organised trip. Of course, some may only be along for the ride, but you knew that anyway, and most disagreements can be sorted out. Economies of scale are an advantage for larger groups; buying in bulk and party discounts can bring costs down considerably if you shop around.

On a commercial trip joining in with a bigger group offers the opportunity to meet more people, more often than not from a diverse background with equally diverse experiences. With a choice of walking companions, each day has variety, and of course the Trek Leader has all the responsibility. Of course put ten or fifteen strangers together under any conditions and there'll be squabbles, and power play, and tears. Especially when tired or under stress. But in a group of ten or so, it's very easy to take a back seat, although it can be incredibly annoying. The greater the number in a group, the greater the odds of having a complete bore, a selfish prat, a moaner, a know all, a constant complainer or a snorer amongst the company. But larger groups cushion the effects of these types, and also increase the odds of there being an absolute gem, a comedian, a flora / fauna expert, a like mind, somebody to play at chess, talk history, read poetry to.

As a trek leader, give me a large group any day. Sure, campsites tend to cover half an acre and the support crew take on the proportions of a small army but the "crack" is always better and there is more to share in the post-dinner conversation. Mornings are the worst time with larger groups, trying to jolly folks on so the day can get started, and decisions tend to be made on behalf of the clients, because ten or fifteen trekkers will rarely agree unanimously when it comes to a vote. Making that choice may alienate you, but it keeps the trekkers sweet with each other - unified against the leader.

GETTING THERE

I once spent some time in an African gaol because one of my clients had a slight visa irregularity. Okay, it was only for one day and they were very pleasant to me but two things did strike me at the time: my client was spending the day beside the pool at the hotel, and beneath the smiles there was definitely the potential for things to turn nasty and for the key to be thrown away.... The business was settled because I had the weight of a large company behind me and more important a good local agent who knew me, the police and the system very well indeed. The agent stuck his neck out because his livelihood, or a great deal of it, depended on it. (And also he was a nice guy. Thank you, Big Mo.) I know this sort of business doesn't happen all the time, and it is an extreme example, but it does highlight some important issues, and provoke a debate on the pros and cons of using a commercial operator.

An independent traveller in my position would have probably been released pretty quickly too, but most certainly with a lighter wallet, and have been reunited with some pretty fraught companions. Good start to a holiday, eh? And even if the imprisonment had been brief, would it have been brief enough not to have upset the trek schedule?

Let's make a detached look at what is involved in organising a trek, regardless of who is organising it.

The local agent

This may seem a strange place to start, but the importance of a good agent cannot be overlooked. Even the biggest names in mountaineering and the most accomplished trekkers use them to lesser and greater degrees. A good agent can, if need be, arrange:

   internal transport for you and your goods
   provide porters, cooks, sirdars and guides
   hire specialised equipment on your behalf
   reconfirm flights and other time-consuming office work
   be your point of contact with home and your embassy
   translate and liaise on your behalf
   provide telephone, faxes and other office facilities
   offer advice and local knowledge
   arrange emergency cover
   book accommodation, food and fuel
   arrange appropriate visa extensions and permits
   find paths through bureaucratic mazes
   bail you out when you get arrested at the airport

It's a fairly comprehensive list but each service has to be paid for. The old adage "You only get what you pay for" definitely comes to mind, and it's important that you find yourself a sound agent so that you do get what you pay for and not get ripped off. Finding an agent can be a trial, the easiest way being a personal recommendation. If you don't know of anyone who has used an agent in the area you intend to visit, seek help through the personal ads in the appropriate periodicals. If that doesn't elicit a response then you could be a bit cheeky and ask around the trekking companies to see who they use.

It's up to you how much you have your agent do for you. You can save in every direction if you are smart and don't mind the hassles. Many of the necessary jobs on the list you can do yourself quite easily, the only cost being time. Time if you have it. Once you have decided on the services required then draw up a contract - signed by all. List everything required and how much you are going to pay for it. Make sure you both have a copy. Do not presume anything will be supplied unless it is written in the contract; verbal agreements are asking for trouble. And don't forget - treat all proposed charges as negotiable. Payment is usually fully in advance from when you meet the agent. Contracts can be drawn up via the post and the fax, but it is unadvisable to pay anything up front other than a small goodwill deposit prior to your departure from home. Don't be pressured into this even if your agent is buying internal flights for you - he will always be able to sell them or get a refund. Sometimes it is possible to retain some of the sum until after the trek as insurance, but this is usually offset by the fact that the agent has your ticket home. Tricky. If you feel your agent has done you a disservice it is very, very hard to get any compensation at the end of your trek...

Initial contact should be made as many months in advance as you can, and it doesn't do any harm to shop around.

CHOOSING AN AIRLINE

Don't let budget dictate who you fly with. What you are paying for is not just flight comfort but security. Aeroplanes get impounded for not paying airport dues, get stranded because they've run out of fuel, get seconded by passing small time Monarchs for personal transport. These planes rarely belong to the big airlines. For a few pounds more you gain a great deal of peace of mind and more power as a consumer, a chance of arriving, the ability to change dates and flight times (very handy), subsidised domestic connections, and flexibility. It can also mean your ticket isn't completely valueless if you miss your flight, which happens regularly. These aspects of your flight are worth much more than the difference between a cheap flight and a quality airline.

Airlines deliberately overbook their flights. They gamble on a certain amount of passengers not checking in to fly. The problem for them is when everyone turns up. The problem for you is when you are the one to be turned away. So make sure you are at the check-in desk in plenty of time. Also, if your baggage is checked in, it makes it very hard for the airlines to oust you. The big companies have agreements between each other and will often fly each other's passengers to help out, which can often work to the customer's advantage, with upgraded service and generally better treatment. It becomes bad news if you have to stay over for another flight. How the companies treat you is amazingly diverse. The worst ones will leave you in the airport all night expecting you to fend for yourself; the best will put you up in the 'Hilton' with a generous allowance to play with.

The poorer airlines often have an underdeveloped PR department and retrospective complaints can fall on deaf, overworked ears. Bear this in mind for when you return to the UK. A good PR department is also handy where luggage, or rather excess baggage is concerned, especially if you are going on a mountaineering or canoeing expedition. A good company should try to meet your special needs and confirm agreements in writing. I've been charged excess baggage because I didn't have a written agreement, and also when I had a written agreement but no flight number on it. Also, if you want excess both ways make sure this is stated on the agreement. Most companies now issue a separate ticket for your excess baggage which helps immensely.

It is only fair to the companies to give them as much notice of your intentions as possible. In return they will usually be more accommodating and helpful.

How much you are charged depends on company policy, your charm, their charm and how much baggage is involved. Prices are usually negotiable which put the airlines in a strong position and you on your knees in your best begging position. Crawling is permitted if it saves you money. Depending on circumstances, airlines will sometimes offer to air-freight excess baggage at a moderate rate on an earlier or later flight, usually if they suspect room/weight is going to be tight on your flight. Not seeing your baggage at the end of a flight for a few hours or days is a nerve wracking experience, the tension being proportional to your faith in the company flying it. How much of a bargain was that ticket?

And should your baggage, whether accompanied or not, fail to join you, what recompense will the airline offer you? These are important questions that must be asked and can be answered for the price of a few phone calls. The travel industry can be a nasty business - many companies accept complaints without thought, many rip people off without conscience or care, accepting bribes and threats as a part of day to day living. The airlines have their culprits too, but most misinformation regarding flights seems to be routed with the travel agent. Yes, one can book direct, but asking the right questions and making sure everything is in writing can ensure clarity whilst still retaining the high street convenience of the TA. Protect yourself by using a ABTA bonded agent (Association of British Travel Agents).

CLAIRE'S STORY

Remember: don't let price dictate your airline. Here is another true story from another intrepid explorer...

"There we sat, early afternoon at Kathmandu Airprt, armed only with a slightly stale croissant, two souvenir laden rucksacks and a sublimely naive faith in Aeroflot, the Russian airline.

Within 24 hours we would be back in Britain bemoaning the weather but appreciating the simple pleasure of a toilet seat after four weeks of squatting.

The plane left on time and apart from the dubiety of the air hostess's sex (due to her over application of make-up and a rather luxuriant moustache) we felt all was well.

The first hint of anything untoward was the sudden unscheduled landing in Calcutta. An announcement was made explaining we were to refuel here since Nepal had low stocks due to flooding.

Next stop was a scheduled one in Dubai. Even by now we were feeling somewhat jaded and the shifting wall of heat which hit us like a furnace door opening was somewhat unexpected since it was the dead of night. We waited here for an hour. Returning to the aircraft we looked forward to the last leg of the journey. However, this was to be the beginning of a 50 hour marathon.

After being airborne for what seemed only minutes we landed again. No announcement was made, let alone an apology, to explain our stop. We disembarked onto Kuwait soil, returning two hours later to find our hand luggage and jackets unceremoniously dumped in the aisle. Our own seats were now gleefully occupied by the middle-eastern equivalent of a drunken stag party.

Separated from Lindsay, my long suffering friend, I eventually found a seat charmingly sandwiched between the increasingly "fragrant" toilet and two inanely grinning Kuwaitis who derived an unnerving amount of pleasure from my blond hair.

As dawn tentatively crept above the horizon we again dipped down to land. Foolishly I assumed this to be Moscow (where we were to await a connecting flight). Having been rudely instructed by the shot-putting hostess to remove ourselves and our belongings, we crossed the tarmac towards a small building noticing that our baggage was also being removed from the hold.

Bewildered, we all huddled quietly together, sure in the knowledge that this most certainly wasn't Moscow. Surrounded by barbed wire and armed guards we watched the Kuwaiti contingency pass through customs. Gradually, a rumour drifted amongst the 64 remaining passengers: they had booked a holiday in a small resort in Russia but their flight had been cancelled. Undaunted they had paid Aeroflot to re-route any flight to accommodate them. Hence our arrival in Sotchi, a Russian backwater on the northern shores of the Black Sea.

We were herded into a waiting room with one stench filled toilet, two benches and barred windows. No formal explanation was forthcoming and for the rest of the four hours we remained in the dark. Why were we not back on the plane and heading for Moscow?

Meanwhile, defying the chaos, we had all unwittingly begun to throng in national groups, the largest of which was French. Although ashamed at my woolly need to flock we found security with a physics teacher from Edinburgh and a sprightly pensioner from Glasgow. The former suffering from Giardia, the latter a severe case of dodging the taxman by travelling the world.

It was not long before a leader made himself apparent. In time a Napoleonic style, rather debonair Frenchman insisted upon information. After much Slavic puzzlement and a tirade of Gallic abuse a woman miraculously appeared who spoke English.

'Nothing to be alarmed about. Your plane has run out of fuel. It may be some time before we can locate any but I'm sure if you're all willing to pay a little each it may speed things along.'

By the time this succinct message was translated into French, the wave of consternation had grown to tidal proportions, the crest of which was a hysterical woman trying to get to Paris for her father's funeral.

The next joke was cracked by a sullen-faced official. We could only leave the confines of this room if we paid $25 for a Soviet visa since, technically speaking, to exit involved a customs check and the trespass of Russian soil! In truth, walking through an aging turnstile into a disused hall.

By the murderous expression on the majority of faces no translation was needed to communicate 'get stuffed'.

A phone call was, however, permitted to an embassy. The British was predictably "unobtained" and the French confessed they had no power to become involved.

The day became interminable. It was only midday and we had been trapped for nine hours already. Ally, our teacher, had begun to vomit blood and the only remedy we could muster were some out-of-date antibiotics prescribed for a tooth abscess.

Sensing the imminent uprising, an offer of dinner at a local hotel was made. There was, however, a catch - we must surrender our passports first.

Foolishly, but in the grips of hunger, we agreed and shuffled slowly through the bureaucratic nightmare of customs control.

Free at last, we were graciously escorted by an armed guard to 'the hotel'

- a guard euphemism for airport canteen. Ah, you may mock but no hint of plastic furniture here. Not even the faintest whiff of curled-corner sandwiches. Suddenly the day took on a surreal quality usually only achieved after a full fortnight of sleep deprivation and a stinking hangover. A set of monstrous wooden doors were opened to reveal a cavernous room. The wooden floor shone with beeswax, reflecting the sunlight pouring through the ceiling-to-floor windows. Draped on each was an extravagant length of red velvet curtain. It was so reminiscent of a grand ballroom we could almost hear the faint sigh of music.

Unfortunately, the meal didn't quite match the decor. We were served luke-warm *bortsch* and a single, sad-eyed fish.

Teased cruelly with the prospect of staying that night in a local hotel but eventually faced with the reality of a disused departure lounge, we all settled down in wartime camaraderie. No-one slept well, even with the snorers relegated to one.

We were awakened by a generous man offering us apples bought at the local market. Perhaps today would be better. We sat and watched planes land and take off. A Norwegian woman somehow managed to buy a ticket on one of them. Having used up every penny she was then refused boarding without a visa (costing $25). Explaining her lack of funds she asked for a refund. Not possible. She returned to the group having paid twice for a flight that still hadn't got her home.

Unexpectedly, that afternoon we were informed we had just enough fuel to get us to another nearby airport to fill up. Reserved in our euphoria, we suspiciously walked onto the tarmac. Those at the front made it onto the plane.

Suddenly a group of soldiers began shouting wildly and barred our entry to the aircraft. After much deliberation and an hour standing in the sweltering heat, we climbed onto the plane. We waited a further three hours for the pilot to collect the cash from the bank to pay for the fuel. He arrived, triumphant, brandishing a carrier bag full of notes. Credit is no longer an option. The introduction of capitalism and its attendant corruption has put paid to that. As the plane took off, two boys surfed in the aisle to the hummed strains of "Surfin' USA". Safety conscious our air hostesses weren't.

We flew up the Volga river to be met with a rather alarming sight. The edge of the approaching runway was littered with the debris from a crashed helicopter, and tottering across the runway, oblivious to the danger, were several middle-aged women wearing headscarves and carrying bulging shopping bags. Where could they possibly be going?

It took seven hours of waiting and endless renditions of every Beatles song known to man before we were refuelled. The heavy presence of military vehicles had sown the first real seeds of concern for our own safety. We hadn't eaten for 12 hours which added to everyone's agitation.

By this time my family had begun to panic. The British Embassy knew nothing and Aeroflot had wiped its flight records 12 hours after departure. They weren't even sure if I had left Kathmandu.

We arrived in Moscow at 3am on Tuesday morning, having left Nepal on the Sunday. Our connecting flight was only four hours off but we still had to endure the wait in the airport hotel. My feet crunched resonantly on the linoleumed floors infested with a million tiny cockroaches. Awakened after only two hours of fitful sleep we were taken to breakfast.

Most of our bedraggled passengers had already dispersed except for a Swiss Budhist whose patient acceptance of fate and rather self-satisfied smile started to wear somewhat thin.

Arriving at Heathrow, the world tilted back on to its axis - nothing more could go wrong....

After almost an hour staring numbly at a squeaking, blatantly empty luggage carousel, I gave up trying to conjure up my obviously missing rucksack. Lindsay guided me to the information desk.

Overwrought, the tears trickled, but my bag was eventually located, languishing in a corner of Moscow airport. I gave up hope of ever seeing it again but British Airways, being the carriers for Aeroflot, ensured it arrived home a week later intact.

Aeroflot avoided paying any compensation, explaining the "incident" as an unavoidable mechanical failure. Our holiday insurance company also wriggled free of responsibility since the delay was homeward-bound.

Lindsay and I recovered, and although my mother and her worry-induced grey hair may not agree, we look back on our journey with "affection"! If only for the crowds this cautionary tale pulls at parties." *Claire Gilchrist*

INTERNAL FLIGHTS

Internal flights often leave you without a choice of either route or operator. The main point here is to ensure your seat is confirmed and double check it is. All international flights should be reconfirmed on arrival in the country of your destination, either personally or by your agent. This involves taking your ticket, passport and possibly a photocopy of both to the airline office. Take a good book too, you may be some time. Often internal flights are cancelled due to adverse weather, insurrection etc, so find out if this happens what will happen to you - will you be put to the front of the queue for the next day, or onto the reserve list? On arriving in Trekland, make reconfirming your flight home a priority. Basically all you have to do is present yourself, your ticket and passport at the airline office, or their agent, to let them know that you have arrived and that you intend to fly home on the date stated. The clerk will then stamp your ticket, there and then confirming your visit, and your seat home. Then do the same with your internal flights. Local agents are very good at this laborious and time-consuming job. In circumstances where it is not possible to reconfirm by phone, you may need to find help: big hotels with confident, local telephonists and fax machines will usually assist, especially if you pay a small "administration fee". Remember, reconfirm right away, and with all airlines. Also if you don't fly, where do you get your rebate? In the country you wanted to fly in, or the country you bought the ticket in? I've heard of people arranging for their internal flight as an integral part of their international flight, ie. the provincial airstrip being named as the final destination rather than the country's major international airport. I've tried this and didn't get away with it, but it doesn't mean to say you won't! Try it!

MAPS AND GUIDEBOOKS
Don't rely on getting guides and maps in the country you intend to visit. Other than the fact that you'll want to spend the preceding rainy winter nights digesting the guides (and maps), specific guides and maps are often easier to obtain in the UK than in the country of origin. Libraries are a good source for both books and maps, although they may need to be ordered. Having a few to look at does give you choice. I do like having a guidebook with me on trek but I don't think my local library would appreciate the condition it returns in.

Guidebooks do vary in their approach so it is worth having a good look at each one. Of course the other good thing about libraries is that they often stock relevant out of print books. Going off on a slight tangent, it is always worth writing to the appropriate tourist board or council for further information on an area. Sometimes this can produce an avalanche of printed matter ranging from leaflets to posters, some of which is surprisingly useful.

Because guidebooks are a specialised sector of the market they tend to be the domain of a few who, for the price of a few stamps, will post you a list of their publications. Decent book shops have wonderful stock lists on computer or microfiche and should be able to help if other suppliers cannot.

Suppliers

Cicerone Press
2 Police Square
Milnthorpe,
Cumbria
LA7 7PY

Nevisport
High Street
Fort William
PH33 6EJ
(01397) 70 4921

Stanford International Map Centre
12-14 Long Acre
London
WC2E 9LP
(0171) 836 1321

Cordee
3A De Montfort Street
Leicester
LE1 7HD
(01533) 543579

New Heights
134 Lothian Road
Edinburgh
EH3 9BG
(0131) 229 2233 (and fax)

Jack Baines
1 Thomas Street
Holyhead
Gwynedd
(01407) 760988

COMMERCIAL OPERATORS

The advantages of using a commercial outfit are manifold. You pay for somebody else to do your research, make your travel arrangements, hire equipment, provide food, book hotels, hire Sherpas, porters, Sirdars, advise you on what to take, keep you well, help you if you are ill, powder your bottom and blow your nose. And then if it all goes wrong phone ABTA, threaten to sue and you get a full refund... Don't quote me. The disadvantages are that you are immediately part of a group, and as such lose the right to lie in bed until you feel like getting up and have virtually no say in changing routes, menus etc. As a member of a group you have a responsibility towards that group and forfeit the right to be selfish, greedy, complaining or late. There is also the chance of spending £2,000 for the privilege of sharing a tent with a heavy snoring, 17 stone, chain smoker. For a month. More of this in 'How to Survive a Trek' later on.

One of the many joys of being a trek leader was working with the people who came on trek, and I have made some very dear friends this way. With so many treks on offer, though, which company do you choose? It's a buyers' market, and if you've got the money all things are just about possible. The good thing about using a commercial operator is that you can largely ignore the previous few sections of this book. By booking onto a commercial trip you bypass a lot of hassle and potential problems, and as I stated earlier, when problems do arise they are somebody else's to handle. Of course they create problems of their own, some not so obvious. With so many companies offering so much it's sometimes very hard to see through the "hype" to view the actual product on offer.

The easiest way to clear the view is to start by asking for a brochure. Even the smallest company should offer detailed, concise, well produced literature, whether its a simple A4 leaflet or a 100 page brochure. The speed with which it arrives can offer a hint about the efficiency of the office. If it's out of print then you should be informed of that. Any literature should have an air of care and organisation about it. Moving on from this you can filter out the ones that don't interest you, usually determined by where you want to go. Also consider disregarding any company that isn't ATOL (Air Tour Operators License) bonded or isn't a ABTA (Association of British Travel Agents) member. Both of these require the company to have a proven track record, and to deposit a substantial part of their turnover as a safeguard to the customer should they go to the wall. ATOL is a legal requirement for any operator that sells any kind of holiday that flies out of the UK, and is government administered. Many companies now have such tiny profit margins that bankruptcy is just over the horizon. Apart from holiday insurance, booking with a bonded company is often a customer's only hope should things go wrong. When ATOL bonding was introduced in 1992 many small trekking companies immediately folded. Others simply based their operation in the country where they led their treks, leaving the customer to make their own travel arrangements to Trekland. Some are very open about this, others disguise it, or try to, with some pretty paltry reasons and patronising, we're-saving-you-money excuses.

Approach the companies again regarding particular trips and ask for further information. They in turn should send a more detailed dossier. The care and efficiency of the office is important as it is often the lynchpin of the whole operation and inefficiency at this level can have a desperate knock-on effect which only manifests itself in the field. Probably when you are there. As with a lot of businesses, employee dissatisfaction often seeps through to the first contact with the public, in this case, the telephonist.

So phone them up and ask a few questions. A proper outfit will encourage this, whether they are large or small. Ask about the trek you fancy doing - if it is a new trip ask if it has been done before. (I'm not joking because I've done it myself. I led a trek that had been created in the office by a non-trekking office worker. I knew it hadn't been done before; unfortunately the twelve people I had with me didn't, a fact that only emerged via their faces as I talked excitedly of going off into the unknown...) To be fair, companies are more open about this these days, and often advertise their recce trips, usually at a reduced rate, as they do have an appeal to a certain kind of person.

Still on the phone, ask who is going to be leading the trip. Even six or nine months beforehand, an organised company should know who is going to be working for them and what trip they are likely to be doing. Despite the image the job often carries, trek leading is hard, sometimes dangerous and often very stressful work. Trek leaders do like working for good companies, good companies being those that keep the hard, dangerous and stressful work to a minimum. So it figures that if you keep seeing the same faces on the leaders'

Twin Otter landing at Lukla airstrip, Nepal - the start to the popular
Everest trek *(Author)*

Rough going on the road to Hushe in Baltistan, Northern Pakistan *(Author)*

A bus in Nepal. Buses like this are common throughout Asia *(Author)*

Crossing a river by yak *(Author)*

page then the company and the leaders are content with each other, which can only be good for the customer. Also ask about your leader's experience and any qualifications he/she possesses, and how many trips they do in a year. Regardless of how good or bad a company is, on trek it's their representative, the trek leader, that often makes or breaks your holiday, and if something goes wrong, whether it's a medical problem, natural disaster or a bureaucratic log-jam, it's up to them to sort it out. And there is no substitute for experience; if you don't have it, the leader should. This is one of the things you are paying for. As for your leader being qualified, this shows that at least he/she has some proven experience and commitment, and has been assessed on this. The current (1995) relevant qualifications, Mountain Leader Certificate (Summer and Winter), Mountain Instructors Award (MIA) and the full guides ticket (Union International de Guides de Haute Montagne - UIGHM) all seem to focus on the European hill walking/mountaineering/climbing scene, and there is no specific Trek Leaders Award, which there should be. Despite the arguments the UIGHM voice in their favour over others, the truth is that none of the current schemes offers formalised training and assessment in altitude and heat-related illness, advanced first-aid, or basic customer care. The most relevant certificate for a trek leader at the moment is a mountain-related first-aid certificate.

In the course of an adventurous trek, the leader will have to draw on skills and experience that range from basic hill walking to high altitude mountaineering, and a leader's "people" skills are as important as any. Ask about leader-to-client ratios and maximum group size. On a climbing trek the ratio should be about 1:2/3 clients, on a trek 1:10, or 15 at the most. I have seen a German group of thirty which had the appearance of a circus and their one leader openly admitted that he didn't know all his clients' names. Is this what they paid for?

A worse situation is when there is no western leader. There is only one reason a company does this and it's cost. Despite technical excellence and a wealth of experience I know of few, if any, non-western leaders. We are a strange breed, with emotions that run from child to saint and back again. In my experience a group without a western leader tends to have a client or clients come forward to try and fill that gap, not always with success or with the full backing of the rest of the group. You can imagine the scene. I have seen some pretty shoddy rope techniques and poor mountain practice amongst western leaders, but unfortunately I haven't seen good techniques or practice with local guides. Of course good local guides exist, but they usually work on the big mountaineering expeditions - big money with big tips, and not on the poorer paid treks. I've said this at the risk of sounding racist, or generalising, but I haven't met another trek leader who hasn't agreed with me, sad that it is.

The more conscientious companies have started training local guides, and hopefully if I revise this book in a few years I'll be able to omit the previous comments.

Next on the telephone hit list is the local agent. As I mentioned earlier local agents are an essential link in the trekking chain. How much the individual uses them is circumstance related. The big companies use them a lot, but the company/agent relationship tends to be a symbiotic affair, after a few years of working together. The independent trekker tends to need the agent more than the agent needs them, which does leave individuals and smaller groups in a rather weak position. Many agents are often only in existence because of the business the commercial outfits give them, and in some cases the agencies have been established by those trekking companies principally to service their needs. So ask the company who their local agents are and how long the company has been using them. Also ask if there are any other subcontractors involved. There are a few trekking firms around who share advertising and common office facilities and you may find yourself booking with one company and travelling with another. Fine, as long as you are told this from the outset. Another trick, particularly applicable on multi-activity holidays, is to have one supplier provide the trekking element, and another the rafting etc. No problem as long as it's well coordinated and the subcontractors are up to standard.

By now you've been on the phone so long that the company's business has ground to a halt, your ear is red hot, BT view you as one of their most valued customers and you've lost all your credibility and any future arguments with your teenage daughter. But before you put the phone down ask just a few more questions. Like what isn't included in the price? Can they accommodate special dietary needs? How many are going to be in your group? Looking through the brochures will probably bring one noticeable difference to your attention - price. Why does one company charge more than another for what appears to be the same basic trip? This is probably due to using different airlines, accompanying leaders and the degree of comfort (hotels, trek goodies etc) you are offered. Economising in this way is fine as long as they are not saving money by cutting down on western leaders. Also ask if you can visit the office and if the company does a slide show. Many companies have an annual promotional tour - showing slides and having guest speakers, competitions etc, and it is well worth going along just to get a feel for the company and the trips they run. Often there is the chance to chat to the staff, and maybe even the leader of the trip you fancy doing. On occasions their talks have the air of a reunion about them and if you are blessed then you'll be able to chin-wag with a client who has been on the trip you want to do. Now this is when the truth comes out! This is the person you want to talk to. For reasons of confidentiality it is unlikely that the company concerned will forward you the name of a previous client, which I respect, but you can appeal yourself via the outdoor press, as per looking for an agent, or at one of their slide shows.

Visiting a company's office can be a real insight - keep your visit brief and let them get on with their jobs. As on the phone, they should be pleasant and informative, even the lowly office junior. After all, if they haven't got an interest in their job how can they do it properly? And if they can't communicate with you, how do they manage with those working in the field, continents apart, joined only by poor phone and tentative fax lines? If something goes badly wrong within the company, these are some of the people who will have to sort it out. And even with the best companies things go wrong - who has control of civil unrest, natural disasters and epidemic illnesses? You should be made welcome in the office for no other reason than the fact that you are a potential customer.

DANGEROUS TRENDS

If all this sounds a touch of an overactive procedure for what is basically booking a holiday, then consider again what kind of holiday it is. Expensive for a start, somewhere in the price region of a good enough used car. Would you buy a car without having some kind of guarantee, or having a very close look at it?

Dangerous, for a second. People get killed on treks. The reasons you don't hear about this is because it usually happens far away from our sensationalising media and it doesn't happen very often. With so many people going trekking it's an inevitability. Keeping it quiet is the proper thing to do to prevent hysteria. However as commercial treks become more adventurous, it's imperative that the company and their employees are competent to operate in these remote, dangerous areas. There is a great rivalry between trekking companies and no one company likes to have a rival advertise a trip that they themselves don't offer. An example of this is the crossing of the Mingbo La in Khumbu, Nepal. This is a high altitude, hard technical route with massive objective dangers. Yet this severe crossing has been belittled by the volume of trekkers who have successfully crossed it, due to the number of operators who promote it. So why do so many companies offer this trip? Because one company did one year, and the others did the next so as not to appear behind the times and lose potential business. I've seen this crossing done very smoothly and as safely as can be expected, but I've also witnessed crossings where I was physically sick because I was convinced I was going to witness a death. The latter is an example of a company running beyond its competence and clearly understaffed. The happy ending to this story is that someone eventually saw the light, stopped using that pass and reversed the trend. So, for your own safety, check out the company.

Because trekking tends to take place in the Third and Developing Worlds, the concept of a holiday, let alone a trekking holiday, definitely belongs to the First World. And yet it is this apparent anomaly that allows trekking operators to work because they rely heavily on cultures where human porterage is a way of life. It is the porters who make treks comfortable (remember comfort!). Because the commercial operators owe so much of their success to the under-rated porter it is only proper that they are treated with the respect they deserve. If you are using porters at all, whether employing them directly yourself, or through a third party, ie. an agent or trekking company, then ensure they are insured, properly paid and equipped to do the job. Some responsible companies do supply their porters with waterproofs, boots, sleeping bags, food and fleeces. Most do not. Will your conscience allow you to watch your porter pass you soaked to the skin, carrying your kit-bag as you slip into your "Goretex" waterproofs - the equivalent of a year's wages?

Finally, how does that company treat the environment? How do they dispose of on-trek rubbish, what kind of toilet facility do they utilise and do they allow the use of wood fires for cooking? As we are privileged to travel in such unspoiled, spectacular country, so we have a moral obligation to maintain it as such.

Articulated yak, Boroghil Pass, Pakistan

It is hard to avoid commercial trekking and the key is to use it to suit yourself. With a bit of experience behind you it's not too hard to design your own trek with your own small group of friends. it's perfectly feasible to book flights through a UK trekking company (a bit more expensive, but look at the security [ATOL]), use their agents to get your permits, hire your crew etc if you need them. Coming via the Big Operator is going to give you credibility with the agent, and you'll be paying a price negotiated in the UK. And the whole thing is to your timetable with the people of your choice. The only way to improve on this, I feel, would be to travel overland to Trekland.

TRAVELLING OVERLAND
It is now possible to drive overland from London to New York, not that I really think the NYPD are going to notice a sharp rise in the number of British registered cars in Brooklyn with the opening of the Channel Tunnel. (And before anyone gets smart, the Bering Sea freezes in winter and it is possible to drive across.) So in theory you could walk, cycle or use public transport to get to Trekland. In fact many do. Walking, cycling and public transport present the fewest bureaucratic problems, usually only requiring a visitor's visa, a receipt proving the bicycle is yours (if appropriate) and proof of means, ie. money. Procuring visas is dealt with later. Real problems abound when taking vehicles overseas. I gather driving through North and South America and Australasia is straightforward, accepting the usual problems of theft-crazy road users, small arms fire etc. In Europe it's relatively easy, and with the end to the Cold War, becoming easier. Security paranoia still seems prevalent in the Middle East although in some sectors things are easing off - Jordan and Iran for example. As for the Far East and Central Asia, whilst their borders are more accessible and becoming increasingly more open, motorised travellers are finding it harder to enter Asia with their vehicles. The main reason is because of efforts by Asian countries to improve the standard of their transport by encouraging their countrymen to buy vehicles of a decent standard - often Japanese, assembled at home. Clapped out 'Transit' vans driven over from Europe fall below standard and deprive the government of any import duties.

Where there is a will there is a way, of course, and many, many people do drive overland - pure adventure in itself.

If you are considering driving any vehicle overland get in touch with the Automobile Association, who can arrange all the necessary paperwork for your vehicle, and then the Royal Geographical Association who have the most up-to-date information about where is reachable, whose borders are shut, and which warring factions are most likely to try and kidnap or kill you and where they are lurking.

Basically what you and your vehicle will require is:

A Pakistani bus

UK Driving Licence
International Driving Permit
Vehicle Registration Document V379
International Certificate for Motor Vehicles
"Green Card" insurance for you / vehicle / 3rd party / trailer
Current Road Tax
Carnet de Passage en Douage

The last item, the Carnet de Passage, allows you to temporarily import your vehicle without having to go through the usual near impossible bureaucracy, or having to pay import duty on it. All the other bits of paper are easily acquired through the motoring organisation. The Carnet de Passage, however, may require leaving a substantial returnable deposit with the AA or a bank at home, who are liable to pay any duties should your vehicle fail to leave the country if entered. This may of course be due to theft, fire, civil unrest or a crafty black-market sale. You may also be arrested for not having your vehicle, so check very carefully with the AA as to what to do should this happen. One couple recently had to leave a £24,000 bond in a British bank in order to secure a Carnet to take a vehicle of that value into China.

One last thing. Make sure all the documents are made out in the name of the driver. If it's a borrowed vehicle, temporarily change the ownership documents via the Dept of Transport (new V379) and avoid a lot of potential problems.

I'm presuming that if you are considering driving a vehicle across continents you'll have a fairly good idea of what is involved. If you haven't then try reading something like *Through Africa - An Overlanders' Guide* by Bob Swain and Paula Schneider (Bradt), just to make you twitch a little. Or whet your appetite!

Ken and Julia Slavin are the masters of overland travel and the official advisers to 'Land Rover' in the expeditionary field. For spares, safety equipment, vehicle modification or shipment, these are the people to get in touch with.

K and J Slavin (Quest) Ltd
Low Pasture Farm
Louth Road
Hainton
Lincs
LN3 6LX
(0507) 313401

USEFUL ADDRESSES

Karakoram Experience
32 Lake Road
Keswick
Cumbria
CA12 5DG
(017687) 73966

Sherpa Expeditions
131a Heston Road
Hounstow
Middlesex
TW5 ORD
(0181) 577 7187

World Wide Journeys & Expeditions
8 Comeragh Road
London
W14 9HP
(0171) 381 8638

Expedition Advisory Centre
Royal Geographical Society
1 Kensington Grove
London
SW7 2AR

Classic Nepal Ltd
33 Metro Avenue
Newton
Alfreton
Derbyshire
DE55 5UF
(01773) 873497

Foreign & Commonwealth Office
Advice to Travellers
(0171) 270 4129
(Political advice)

BBC 2 Ceefax Page 564 onwards
Current advice to travellers

CHAPTER TWO

Passports, visas and money

So you know where you want to go, and when. You've booked the time off work, sweet talked the spouse and you're just counting the days till you leave. The kids are in kennels and the dog's at your mum's (who thinks that you're mad...) so relax. Well, not quite.

PASSPORTS
You won't go far without an up-to-date passport. For couples travelling together I think it is best to have separate passports. Should the worst come to the worst then you will be able to travel independently - I'm not referring to you falling out, but if one is evacuated due to illness there is no guarantee that the other can accompany them.

One year visitors' passports are becoming very out of fashion these days, and many countries will no longer accept them. Avoid any problem by getting a ten year passport - they are still good value. Application forms can be found in main post offices, with a note of your nearest passport office. Phone them up and ask how long it will take to process your application. Add three months for your own peace of mind. I must add here that the Passport Offices I've dealt with have been superb and couldn't have been more helpful, so don't be afraid to phone. Remember, you can apply to any office for your passport, not only the closest. The minimum expiry of a British passport is 10 years for a full passport and 3 years for a visitors' passport.

If you already have a passport check the expiry date. Save yourself a desperate struggle at the border/embassy/airport by making sure your passport doesn't run out half way round your trek, or half way across the Atlantic. In fact make sure it doesn't run out until you've been home at least a month. Why? Because you might be delayed... hospitalised? imprisoned? It happens every week, every day, to someone, somewhere. I've heard horrific stories of travellers trying to renew passports and extend visas from hospital beds. Also make sure there are at least five or six blank pages left so there is enough space to allow all the little men in uniforms to stamp and sign and stick on the extras, eg. entry stamps, exit stamps, trekking permits, customs declarations etc, etc. And in the case of Pakistan - your liqueur permit number and the declaration that you are an alcoholic.

Never underestimate how close to the letter most customs and immigrations officers will stick when faced with a passport or visa irregularity or abnormality. For two reasons. One, the officer has fought hard to secure his present position, and will do nothing to jeopardise his secure government job or his promotion prospects by being in any way out of line. Two, the officer is on the make and knows that no matter how or who you protest to, if your paper-work is not up to it, you are going home. In other words by playing by the rules he has the upper hand and will only relieve you in exchange for a wad of notes.

For travelling in the EC a UK passport is all you need to cross freely from country to country. Handy because some of the best trekking in Europe is in and around the mountains that form the most natural borders. The newer EC passports are practical, and universally accepted. They certainly zip into trouser pockets easily, and don't seem to become dog-eared so quickly. The down side is that the integral bar code on the back gives governments, including our own, too much information too quickly, and that additional information can easily be added without us knowing. Paranoid? Squad cars in Germany have on board computer terminals that allow the officers access to all manner of details from how much tax you've paid to where your father was born simply by running your ID card through their machine. And remember, you don't own your passport - it belongs to HM Government. From a more practical point of view, the EC passport, being smaller, gets used up quicker - embassies and government agencies using whole rather than part pages to place visas, entry stamps etc. If you plan to travel a lot you can ask for extra pages in your passport, 96 as opposed to the usual 30. It will cost a few pounds extra, and is only available as a UK passport and not in brown EC trim. Definitely the thing to have, especially if it's full... The other type of passport to have is a blue UN passport. If you have one then skip the next section on Visas.

VISAS

Apart from your passport you may be required to have a visa and to show proof of your means, ie. cash, travellers' cheques and/or credit cards.

International Visas are the original Calvinistic pleasure - they are the keys to heaven gained only through patience, perseverance, hard work and often considerable sums of money. We in the UK are often regaled with tales of visitors stranded at our airports being denied entry because of lack of visas. Usually around Christmas time by a news-starved sensationalizing media. I wonder if other countries show the same thing on television because judging by the stories I hear regarding visas, the UK immigration department are mere beginners at this game. And judging by the amounts of cash needed to sort out visa 'irregularities', amateurs in a professional world.

Always leave the UK with the appropriate visas to avoid becoming a bit part actor in some foreign regional news item. Never rely on buying a visa at the border. Another advantage in gaining a visa in the UK is that it can work out considerably cheaper. At present this is how the Nepalese government system works. Visas issued in the UK are usually for up to a 29 day period from the day you enter. Extensions are possible, on production of exchange receipts proving you have changed $20 for every day you wish to extend your visas by - minimum one week. The Nepalese government will issue visas at the border but only for two weeks, so you will have to change $280 to be able to stay 22 days. No problems if you are organising your own trip and paying up front - but if you have paid for your trip in the UK through a commercial outfit, you'll have to buy a lot of cakes to spend those rupees. Of course it's a currency virtually worthless outside Nepal. The extension costs $10 to administer and two (if you're lucky) days to process. You can have your agent do it for you, but again you pay. This system is being adopted by other countries in similar forms, principally to make a fast buck and secondly to keep people in the country just long enough to spend their money. Nobody wants low budget travellers any more. Unfortunately, the visa issuing departments of some embassies are a good reflection of the inefficiency and corruption that hinders the progress of the country they represent, and gaining that desperately sought after visa can be a real trial of patience. Allow at least three months for the process. Seriously.

The initial move to gaining a visa is to apply, in writing, for an application form. If you receive a letter in reply stating that you don't need a visa, then carry that letter in your passport - official letterheads can often produce respect, if not action, should there be a borderline contradiction. Should there be a dispute then quote the ambassador's name frequently implying there is a connection... best of luck.

If you are a member of HM Forces, clearance must be gained from your commanding officer prior to application.

When the application arrives study it carefully, and make a photocopy as a reserve. Try to answer the questions honestly and don't get smart. One problem may arise under 'occupation'. The good news is that if you are a teacher or doctor (of anything) you will gain instant respect. (Apart from in the UK). Don't declare if you are unemployed, or a journalist of any kind. If you are one of the latter, bury your press card deep in your baggage.

For your address in the country you intend to visit, that of a quality hotel usually suffices. Where possible go for a visitor's as opposed to a business visa, and always, always check to see if you need a single, double or multiple entry visa.

Always allow at least two extra days for late flights when asked how long the visa is for. Remember a month is four weeks, 28 days as opposed to 31.

Photocopy your completed form for reference, should there be a problem with your application later on. Many Asian embassies have a great mistrust of our banking systems and may insist on payment by Postal Order. Just do as you're told. You'll also be required to enclose numerous passport photos. I wonder what happens to them all? Anyway, do this and get a few extras to take away with you - four should do. Always, always, always send your passport by registered post. Most embassies will return it likewise. (Most! It's a gamble.) There are several ways of speeding things up. One is to go direct to the visa section of the appropriate embassy and go through the whole process there and then. Many will process your application overnight and you can collect your passport and visa personally next day. Handy, if you have the time and live in London where most of the embassies are. Check that embassies will do this or you could be in for a wasted journey, as anyone who has been to the Iranian or Saudi Arabian Embassy on spec will testify. Take an outline of your planned visit with you with places, dates and accommodation arrangements, as questions may be asked.

In the visa section be polite but firm and try and avoid confrontation. I've never been asked for a bribe in the UK, but I had a friend who had a visa office worker invite himself to lunch which speeded up his application. I have had demands for extra photos, photocopies of birth certificate and told to fill in forms in duplicate, duplicate. You just do it, keep smiling and look forward to the day you get a diplomatic passport. Being treated with complete indifference and/or rudeness abounds but don't lower yourself to the same level or your application will suddenly lower itself down the queue too. Stay cool.

If you can't, then pay a professional to do it for you. Established initially to serve the business community, there are now several agencies in the market who will arrange visas for the leisure (ha!) traveller. You sign the appropriate forms (which they give you), a cheque (which you give them), leave your passport in their capable hands and leave them to take the hassle. Brilliant, and, I feel, well worth the money. if you are after several visas then it can work out a bit on the pricey side, though in many cases still cheaper than flying to London to sort it out.

The cost of visas ranges from free to (more usual) prohibitively expensive. Often it's because we're British, and the fee we have to pay reciprocates the fee we charge others for the privilege of the right to visit us. The fees we charge are thinly veiled deterrents, to try and minimise poor Asian visitors. I'm only glad we don't have to go through the same administrative procedures to gain our visas from them. This involves numerous interviews, examining of accounts, references, the whole works. Multi-entry visas again push up the cost but pay and be grateful. If, on your journey to Trekland you have to stop off overnight or make a transfer in some other country, even if using only one airline, check carefully if you need a visa for those few hours you will be there, especially if you are there after midnight, as your visit will then be classed as two days. You may be classed as being in transit and be allowed to retire to a hotel for a night, leaving your passport as security.

You may be required to have a visa, in which case failure to have one may result in you not getting on board the plane, not being allowed off the plane, sent back to where you've just come from (who won't let you in because you've no visa) or forced to buy a visa for lots of money... another nightmare scenario. Check with the appropriate consul and the airlines to make double sure, and sleep easy.

MONEY
You can't buy happiness. I've tried renting it on several occasions and I'd be hard pressed to try and deny that I wasn't momentarily a pretty happy chap. One thing's for sure though, without money you're not going to go far, and if you do you're not going to feel very secure or warm, or well fed. The rotten thing about money is that it is very handy stuff to have, and for most of us, hard to come by. Carrying lots of it around inter-continental is not so clever, offering the opportunity to make someone (the villain) a have, and you (the victim) a have not. And insurance companies are not very good at paying out for lost or stolen cash.

The other issue with money is the amount you need, or may need. Maurice Herzog had three porters carrying the silver coins he needed to pay for his expedition to Annapurna, but in this day and age that should be quite unnecessary.

First off we have the travellers' cheque. This allows you to spend as little or as much as you need or want to, the unused cheques being valid for your next trip away or simply cashed for their sterling value when you return. The cost of their printing and the process of their administration is born by you, by means of a small commission, usually 1-5 per cent of this purchase, but included in that is insurance cover. This means that stolen, lost or damaged cheques will be replaced at face value free of charge - most on your return, but some, like Thomas Cook, or American Express to name but two, will replace them, within two days, to you, abroad. Don't wait until you lose it to find out how to claim replacements. Make sure you put your signature on each cheque in the bank when you buy, because if you have any unsigned cheques they are not insured. You have to countersign them again when you go to cash them. And of course, that is the travellers' cheque's disadvantage, you have to have somewhere to cash them. No problem in most cities as major banks and tourist hotels will accept them readily, taking, of course, the customary commission, and exchange rates. Dollar cheques are most readily acceptable.

More accepted locally, especially by switched-on businessmen, is hard cash, dollars, Deutschmarks and pounds sterling. If you play by the rules then you will still do well, the exchange rate usually being more favourable for hard currency, and you will receive an exchange receipt (remember your visa extension) which will keep your nose clean with the authorities. Those without the need for exchange receipts, who are perhaps trekking on a limited budget and would benefit from a more favourable exchange rate, have another option, the Black Market. In virtually all the countries of the world this kind of deal is illegal, but widespread. The punishment for being caught differs and despite how casual and commonplace Black Market money-changing has become, it is still illegal and to be caught leaves you guilty and at the mercy of the powers that be.

I am not advocating illegal trading but if you do decide to exchange money on the street then some words of advice. Decide before entering negotiations how much you want to change and separate that amount from the rest of your funds and keep it to hand. Negotiate the rate prior to revealing how much you want to change, just to see how far your dealer will go. If the dealer doesn't have the cash on him, and won't do an immediate transaction, then call off the deal. Try and make your deal as public as possible without drawing too much attention to yourself - a quiet seat in the corner of a cafe for example. Don't go off down back streets or into houses, and try, where possible, to have someone else with you. Preferably a large prop forward or a doberman. See the money you are changing, and count it yourself before handing over yours. The dealer will know that you are unlikely to run off with his loot, the opposite can never be assumed.

Credit cards are becoming more and more popular with travellers, a sign of how the times are changing and a mark of the increase in wealth of your average holidaymaker. They offer the comfort of having the option of fairly sizeable amounts of cash to hand without actually having to carry it around, or pre-paying for the option as in travellers' cheques. Whilst not so convenient up-country, in most main towns on the five continents, major needs can be met either by paying directly with plastic, or by using it to buy travellers' cheques or draw funds at large banks. Write to your card-issuing agency (your bank!) for details of where your card is acceptable - give them a clue by telling them where you intend to go. Visa, Access, American Express and Mastercard are all pretty much acceptable throughout the world. Having sung their praises don't rely on them as your only source of funds. If you are using your card to pay for goods or services direct then be ultra-careful, making sure that the docket has been filled in correctly, and that the sum stated is correct and that figures cannot be added to it after you have signed. And, of course, keep all your receipts. Note also the emergency number so your card can be cancelled in the event of it being stolen.

(**Editor's note:** China - as always - is a special case. Many shops, even 'posh' ones, still cannot accept credit cards, and banks won't either. Traveller's cheques may only be redeemable at one bank in the town - and they may have run out of the ever necessary bureaucratic 'forms'.)

Lorry on the road to Kashgar, China

CHAPTER THREE
Security and insurance

SECURITY

Be sure that if someone really wants to steal your gear they will! However, most thefts are acts of opportunity rather than deliberation, and by removing the temptation you have immediately lessened the risk. It may not occur to you how valuable your kit is. Of course it is expensive to buy back home, but in the Third World its price becomes almost obscene. What most of us carry in our rucksacks amounts to several years' wages for whole families in Trekland and it's no wonder it gets stolen. Without realising it many of us rub poor people's noses in it by walking around dangling the marks of that aforementioned wealth from our baggage and bodies. I'm talking about cameras, watches, jewellery, designer jeans etc. So we create resentment between ourselves and our hosts.

A good start, therefore, would be to dress down and adopt a lower profile. Start by trying to keep as much as you can inside your rucksack or your pockets. Cut down on expensive jewellery too. Wearing too much local jewellery is a bit of a giveaway as well. You probably paid too much for it and you'd be as well wearing a T-shirt that says 'I'm a sucker for local rubbish - hassle me!' Don't flash your money around, and don't keep it all in one wallet or purse. Split it up. Here's a system I use and it must be good because I'm Scottish, ye ken. I keep a smallish amount of cash in small used bills (force of habit) in my wallet which I keep in my pocket. To avoid it being picked I have a strong cord attached to my wallet, which in turn is tied to a belt loop on my trousers. It also stops you leaving it behind on shop counters. A posh version of this would be to use elasticated shock cord instead. A good return for your money! Travellers' cheques, further cash, passport and other goodies I keep in a soft-backed pouch under my T-shirt hung round my neck. Under loose clothing it doesn't look like an inspection hatch screwed to my front. It also has the advantage of not getting in the way of rucksack hip belts or being left behind in the loo - something that marsupial pouches can be guilty of.

Little kangaroo pouches - "bum bags" worn back to front, looking like a Shakespearian codpiece - are very much in vogue these days. There is no doubt they are very handy, especially if you are a baby kangaroo. They are easily entered, and removed, particularly by small doe-eyed children, in a scam common throughout the world. Whilst older taller children plead with you, stopping your progress, by either out and out begging or trying to sell you something, sometimes off a tray pressed to your mid-riff, their smaller kin are under those outstretched arms in and at your goodies. Or they are working in pairs - one stops you, the other comes in from behind, releases the buckle, and before your pouch has a chance to fall is snatched by the other and they are off almost before you realise what has happened.

I have also stashed cash and a few travellers' cheques in my rucksack. This was enclosed in a polythene bag and slipped down into the internal pocket that holds the 'Fformat' in place in my sack. My rucksack weighed so much, I reckoned that if I was mugged, my attackers wouldn't be able to run off with it and I'd still have some emergency cash. Sadly though, I'm sure it has happened many times.

Another backup for particularly thin extras, ie. large currency notes, is the good old-fashioned money-belt which can be worn quite discretely. Don't buy a nylon one because they are sweaty, and then they start to smell. A good thin one shouldn't interfere too much with waistline activities.

Rucksack security is a problem, and the more zips and pockets the bigger the problem. Try and keep the more valuable and stealable bits buried deep within, so if someone opens the top it isn't immediately Captain Hook's treasure chest. Small padlocks are available - they are very cheap - that allow zips to be locked. I have mixed feelings about them, only really using them when putting my rucksack in the plane, and then as much to stop accidental openings or opportunist thieving by baggage handlers. On trek and in the city I feel they draw unwarranted attention to your sack - what is so special about that rucksack that it has to be locked? Thieves are not going to pick a padlock - they'll just use a razor blade and open your bag the quick way. A real inconvenience being left with a half empty damaged rucksack as opposed to a half empty usable sack. Razoring rucksacks seems to have been a bit of a sport in South America for a while, the only defence being a roll of expanded aluminium mesh inside as a liner - an inconvenience justified if the sport goes through a revival. You will also become the centre of attention at the airport as your sack goes through the x-ray machine. The best prevention is not to leave it unattended - have a friend sit on it or alternatively chain it to a Rotweiler (don't leave any raw steaks inside and take your packed lunch with you).

For dodging around town and hiding your expensive gear, a small daysack is ideal. If I'm on a photographic mission I use a different system - see Chapter Seven.

I confess to leaving valuables in my hotel room when I am about town, a bit silly really, but I do stay in good hotels, usually with people I know. Thefts from hotels are quite common and hotel management are very reticent to take action because of the adverse publicity that two big policemen create standing in the hotel lobby. They are also embarrassed to have to admit that their security is not 100 per cent as it is likely that the theft was an inside job. Hotel strong boxes have a better reputation as have left luggage facilities - just make sure you get a receipt for any bags left behind, and that they are locked. Trying to get back into two key strong boxes can, on occasions, be a test of patience. The duty manager who hold the other key will inevitably be on holiday, or day off. Of course nobody else will know where the keys are. I had one colleague who had to have a hotel strong box opened with an oxy-acetylene torch. A bit worrying as her passport was inside, and she was due to fly home in two hours.

Don't lose those keys. One or three keys are fine in your 'round the neck' pouch. But by the time you've added your house keys, car keys, drawbridge keys etc, you'll end up walking like Quasimodo with a chest that looks as if it's about to produce an alien. 'Lowe' incorporate a little dog clip inside the top pocket of a lot of their rucksacks and bum bags for clipless rucksacks. Bet the neighbours will be impressed that your car keys have been round the Khumbu or up to 21,000ft. Better to leave them behind if you can.

Passports and airline tickets, again, are best left behind if possible. As you have to reconfirm your flight, why not have your agent do it, and give him the responsibility of your ticket and passport. Always, always have a photocopy of your essential bits and pieces: your airline ticket, insurance documents and the relevant bits out of your passport - the page with your photo and birth details, and a copy of the page with the appropriate visa. Also make a note of your passport number, date of issue and expiry and where it was issued. I don't know why either, but I've had to give it to officialdom in every continent I've travelled in at some juncture. Have a few photocopied passport details spares to give away if you want to impress the local police. On the same note make a copy of your insurance reference number and the company's 24 hour contact phone number. Just do it and I'll explain why later. And should the worse come to the worst - a card with your next-of-kin details and organ donor cards if appropriate.

Someone else who should be interested in your details, but isn't always, is your local branch of Her Majesty's Government, ie. the British Embassy. If you have no other person in the country you are walking in who knows where you are going, and how long you are going to be gone for then pop along to your local embassy and register with them. Or try to. I've tried to on several occasions and I've been treated with complete indifference. If you succeed then they might want a copy of your passport details, your itinerary, flight details, insurance documents and a passport photo. If I was in a country by myself then I would insist they did this.

INSURANCE

Now, if you aren't aware of the need for insurance then you only need pick up the *Yellow Pages*, phone the first number under insurance and have your ear melted. What may not appear so obvious is what kind of cover you are looking for.

If you are travelling on a trip with a commercial company then they will inevitably offer you an insurance package along with the holiday. By and large they are very much the same, pretty good, and policies designed for trekkers. Most will insist on some cover, the danger for them being if something goes wrong with you and you are not insured, they'll end up picking up the tab. But get even by insisting you have cancellation cover, so that if the company goes bust, you won't. Make sure it covers you for cancellation due to illness too, because this happens often, and that the cover extends to your spouse and dependants too - their illness may necessitate you cancelling your holiday. Still under personal cover, make sure life and limbs are worth a fixed price, and that you are covered for any time you cannot work because of illness or, shiver to think, invalidity. Whilst thinking of illness make sure your cover extends to rescue and medical bills in Trekland - this can be very expensive. Any time I've been insured for trekking and mountaineering it has stated this on the cover note, in big letters! Make sure yours does too. Read the small print very carefully, or you could be seriously out of pocket. As for your equipment, insurers will always argue how much a piece of lost or stolen equipment is worth, even if they haven't seen it. Unless, of course, it has been insured at replacement cost, ie. not insured for the worth of the piece, but how much it will cost to replace. In some circumstances, cameras for instance, this is often much more than the original purchase price.

Possessions should be covered for loss, theft and damage. If they are lost or stolen then try and get a police statement to that effect. I say 'try' because police forces throughout the world find this simple request a big headache. I suspect one reason is because the poor bobby has to extract a statement from a foreigner who inevitably doesn't speak his language.... Another is because many people put in false claims as means to a small insurance rebate. But try anyway, and be patient if the police are a little grumpy. I had a friend who had his ski boots stolen from his hotel and after reporting the theft to the local police, had his hotel room searched in his absence by a detective. Be warned. If the police do take a statement they can be very thorough, even aggressive, if they suspect you are trying to make a false claim. Or they may choose to ignore you, or tell you to come back later, make an appointment next week - anything in fact to deter you so that they do not have to fill out a form and run the ever so slight risk of being accountable later, either to their superiors or the insurers. They must give you a copy and/or sign and stamp your claim form (which you have with you...). Your insurance company should enclose an instruction sheet on how to claim from them when something does go wrong. Another reason that a police statement may be hard to acquire could be the lack of a police force, or illiterate policemen. In either case your next recourse is to try your trek leader or your agent and see if they can give you a cover letter, preferably on headed notepaper, to send off with your claim. I know this can sometimes satisfy insurers. If your trek leader does this for you, tell him/her to make a copy for their own personal files in case the insurers check up with them later...how do I know this? Just ask me.

Other things to look out for - is your insurance valid for the country you are going to? Don't laugh, because deep in the small print there are often clauses that exclude certain countries. Is your baggage covered whilst in transit? Are you insured if your return is delayed? In fact will they compensate if there is a delay at either end of your journey? I think an air-traffic controllers' strike is justification for booking into a very posh hotel. Better to extend your cover by a few extra days or a week, just in case you are late getting home...or if your bags decide to take a different flight. Is your cash insured, and if so, for how much hard currency are you covered? This is important, because you may find yourself forced to carry large amounts of cash to pay porters etc. You'd only need to fall into a stream to be in big trouble come pay day for the boys or when your next "Visa" payment is due. Most porters I've known would be singularly unimpressed if you tried to pay them with a Royal Bank of Scotland cheque...

Shop around for insurance as prices can vary considerably. As with flights, insurance can sometimes be arranged via the big trekking companies - even if you are not going on one of their trips. I suspect that they are on commission. And why not, everyone has to earn a crust. Here is the kind of difference we are talking about: two quotes for a four week trip in Nepal, climbing Mera Peak. High Street Travel Agent - £126.00. Trekking Company - £75.00.

Should the worst happen, and you have to make a claim, do so as soon as possible. The first thing the insurers will ask for is your policy number. Pencil a note of it, and the 24 hour emergency number in the back of your passport. More of these details later under "Emergency".

If your insurers are not up to scratch, and you feel you have cause for complaint, and you've taken that complaint as far as you can with the insurers then there is an insurance ombudsman, as your next level of complaint.

Insurance cover check list
Make sure you are covered for at least the following:
Medical
Medical Treatment   -   Illness
                                 -   Accident

Air Ambulance	Personal Liability
Hospital costs and allowance	Equipment
24hr Emergency Service	Legal Expenses - should you need to sue
International Rescue	Baggage and Personal Effects
Search and Rescue	Money and Travellers' Cheques
Personal Accident/Disablement	Cancellation/curtailment
	Passport Indemnity
	Missed Departure
	Travel Delay

Particular Sport - eg. mountaineering, rock climbing or white water rafting.

Get in touch with these people and talk about your insurance needs. These names are given without prejudice, but they did give the most speedy and civil answers to my questionnaire. Another nine didn't even reply....

Bishopgate Insurance Ltd
Bishopgate House
Tollgate, EastHigh
Hampshire
SO53 3YA
(01703) 644455

P.J. Hayman & Co Ltd
Forestry House
New Barn Road
Burriton, Nr Petersfield
Hampshire
GU31 5SL
(01730) 260222

Campbells Irvine Ltd
48 Earls Court Road
Kensington
W8 6EJ
(0171) 937 6981

And if need be...
Insurance Ombudsman Bureau
31 Southampton Row
London
WC1B 5HJ
(0171) 928 7600

Insurance is also available to members of the British Mountaineering Council. They offer a good cover, particularly if you intend to climb. Their prices are a bit steep but are on a sliding scale and become more reasonable if you are going out on an extended tour. They can be contacted at:

BMC
177-179 Burton Road
West Didsbury
Manchester
M20 2BB
(0161) 445 4747

It is hideous to presume that your service crew do not need insurance when you do, especially considering that an accident for them could mean a complete loss of earnings and for the livelihood, not only of them but their families.

Insurance for your porters is therefore advisable and in instances compulsory, government subsidised and easily arranged either through local agents or government tourist departments. Ask at the consulate; it is usual to arrange cover for numbers, rather than the names of crews, prior to hiring. This allows one to move up country knowing that you have cover for your porters, even if you haven't a clue who you are going to hire. When you do hire, their names and details, taken from National ID, must go down on the form with their signatures or the insurance is invalid.

If you have an agent, or Sirdar hiring on your behalf, ask to see the insurance certificate (make out it's just your western curiosity getting the better of you) before you go trekking. The point about Sirdars dodging paying insurance is how little they pocket - it is very cheap indeed to arrange cover.

CHAPTER FOUR
Pre-trek health and fitness

"Look to your health and if you have it, praise God, and value it next to a good conscience; for health is the second blessing that we mortals are capable of; a blessing that money can't buy."
Izaak Walton (1593-1683). The Complete Angler.

"One cannot sweat and worry simultaneously."
Alastair Borthwick.

Health and fitness are a lot of what trekking is about and being without either on trek is going to lessen considerably the quality of that trip. They are related terms, as different treks require different levels of both, but being without either is asking for trouble. Apart from the obvious advantages of being able to arrive in camp during daylight and not falling asleep in your soup, being fit and remaining healthy have numerous hidden advantages, and being without either can have tremendous detrimental knock-on effects.

Fitness and health are very closely linked, and it is rare to have the former without the latter. On trek the connection twixt the two becomes very apparent and one realises how reliant fitness is on health and vice versa. It is you who walks the trek - poor preparation equals poor performance, equals negative experience. In other words, your misery and discomfort preoccupy your thoughts, your holiday is ruined and you would be as well sitting on a bus as being out in Trekland. Your mental health and wellbeing are linked inextricably to your physical health. Some people manage to remain mental athletes on trek in spite of poor physical health but they are few and far between, and it a dangerous folly to presume that you are one of them. Time and time again I have watched people on trek slink into a downward spiral of depression because they have been hit by some tummy bug, heat-stroke or toothache. The focus of their attention is centred on their own misfortune as the grandeur of the situation goes by unnoticed.

This is to be avoided at all costs and the way forward is to become fit and healthy long before you go on trek and to keep it through careful preparation, prevention or cure whilst you are out there. We all succumb to ailments on occasions; being fit helps to speed up recovery.

Best having a dental check-up before going on trek -
dentist in Peshawar, Pakistan

FITNESS

I am trespassing into other's territory and, judging by the number of books on the subject, quite a lot of people's territory. But I'll throw in my tuppence worth anyway because I haven't found a fitness book designed specifically for trekkers. Being fit is a good feeling - that feeling being produced by a morphine-related chemical called endomorphine. It is possible to become an endomorphine junkie, as has happened to a few compulsive runners. However, we won't use that as an excuse to flop back down on the couch and switch on the television, so here are a few thoughts and pointers on becoming trek-fit. But they are only pointers and must be backed up by proper research and a well designed fitness programme. Physiologically we are all basically the same animal, but we each have our strengths, weaknesses and biological idiosyncrasies so a personal fitness programme must be just that - personal.

Before we don our trainers and Alf Tupper vests - think more slowly. Trying to get fit in a hurry is not going to work. Allow yourself six months to achieve that fitness, if it happens in four just think of it as a bonus and enjoy those other two months as a fit person. Trying to get fit in a hurry will only create a new set of anxieties, tire you out quickly and increase your chances of sustaining an injury.

Rest and sleep are as important as exercise. Train twice or three times a week maximum unless you are on a special programme, and rest between sessions. Go to bed early and get lots of Zzzzz's. Your body needs that time to recover and grow. Fuel it with sensible foods (taken regularly), stop smoking and indulge in other vices with moderation. Sex seems to be okay but watch out for muscle strains, and don't lose too much sleep...

So, thinking of our common elements let's start our exercises by looking at the source of our motive being: our heart and lungs, the cardiovascular system. As any eight year old doctor will tell you, our heart pumps blood to our muscles. This blood supplies, amongst other things, oxygen, taken via the lungs, which our muscles need to enable them to do their stuff. A poor supply of oxygen is the result of overworked muscles or an inefficient heart and lung set-up. If you can't manage to avoid this then you are considered to be working below the Aerobic Threshold. Aerobic fitness is endurance. So, we really want to work on that, for starters (just try and dismiss the image of lycra-clad bodies bounding around to loud music).

The tender heart, I am constantly assured, is a muscle just like our others, and like those ones that let us lift pints of beer and use our bare hands to open bags of Tortilla Chips. With the proper exercise, our hearts can actually be made stronger and become developed. Unlike other muscles, if it is overworked or damaged then there is a tendency for us to fall over and die. Only once mind you.

Train don't strain

...or you know what will happen. Set a red line on your heart's rev counter with this simple formula for your training pulse. By working at this level for 20-40 minutes at a time, your aerobic fitness will progress, as directed in the aerobic training schedule later on.

Allow your pulse to drop as near to your rest pulse, as possible, and at least below 100 before you raise it once more. There doesn't appear to be any advantage in more than two of these sessions a day, even if you are working within your Training Pulse maxims. Exercising at a pulse rate higher than your recommended TP will soon put you into oxygen debt, which leads to lactic acid buildup in the muscles, discomfort, training set-backs and all sorts of bother....

To work out your max pulse, take 220 minus your age. Eg. for a 30 year old, a max would be 190. To work at, say, 70 per cent would be:

$$\frac{(220 - 30) \times 70}{100}$$

Here is a three month aerobic training schedule for beginners. Adapt it to suit yourself, and if you find three sessions a week too much then lengthen the rest time in between them from say two to three days.

WEEKS 1-3

Session 1	20 mins at 65% max level heart rate
Session 2	20 mins at 65% max level heart rate
Session 3	20 mins at 70% max level heart rate

WEEKS 4-6

	Session 1	2 x 10 mins at 75% max level heart rate
	Session 2	20-30 mins at 65% max level heart rate
	Session 3	20 mins at 70% max level heart rate

WEEKS 7-9

	Session 1	2/3 mins x 5 mins at 80% max level heart rate
	Session 2	30-40 mins at 65% max level heart rate
	Session 3	20-30 mins at 70% max level heart rate

WEEKS 10-12

	Session 1	3/4 mins x 3 mins at 65% max level heart rate
	Session 2	30-40 mins at 65% max level heart rate
	Session 3	20-30 mins at 65% max level heart rate

if this is too much bother for you it can be reduced to:

BEGINNERS -   Work for 30x20 mins sessions per week for 3 months at 60%.

INTERMEDIATE -   After the above, do the same again only at 70%.

ADVANCED -   Do all the above, then another three months at the max, training pulse rate at 85%.

There are many forms of exercise that push the body aerobically that can be introduced easily into most lifestyles. Some may exist already, such as trekking's parents - hill walking and mountaineering. Fine if you are able to get out every weekend. There is no doubt that walking on the hills is the best way of getting fit for walking on the hills, and should figure very strongly in any training programme. If for no other reason than making sure your boots do not cause any physical discomfort/injury. However, even those who spend lots of time on the hill resort to supplementary exercise.

Cycling is a great exercise, not only increasing aerobic capacity but also increasing strength to boot. Despite what the old road men of the last decades say, gears are the thing and a bicycle with 18 or 21 speeds is not over-geared. The aim of cycling is to keep your legs spinning at a constant 60-120rpm - keeping up your aerobic rate but not putting strain on your legs. Cyclists call it the Rate of Cadence. Use your gears to try and keep it constant. Toe clips allow you to pull the pedal up as the opposite leg pushes down, increasing your efficiency and building muscle. Cycling does make you stiff though, so always follow a hard session with a good, long gentle stretch afterwards. The wide arm stance and the forward lean allow you to draw plenty of breath into lungs that are comfortably suspended within your rib cage. Knees are spared a pounding because your bottom is supporting your upper-body weight and the geometry of the bicycle and its air filled tyres are absorbing much of the shock.

Often on treks, people arrive never having walked a great deal before. Most are fit enough, but the ones I've seen who've adapted the best have been cyclists. It is my preferred exercise because in one hour I can cover so much ground, I'm high enough up to see over hedges, cars etc, and I can zip through rush hour traffic to work having saved time, taken some exercise and added nothing to air pollution or road wear. Wear a helmet and make sure your bicycle is set up correctly for you - the correct saddle and handle bar heights and angles are crucial in allowing you to gain the maximum from your cycling and avoiding injury. Don't be in too much of a hurry - like any other form of exercise. Start and finish with some stretching and break into your bike routine slowly. Cycling will make you a better driver too, or it should, because as a cyclist you'll become aware of the bad manners of many car drivers.

Running

In the '70s and '80s the popularity of jogging and running grew to proportions that no other sport had ever done before or has done since. Millions of people fell victim to jogging in People's Marathons/Half Marathon fever. Only the minority competed in more than one or two events, but the commitment of time and energy involved in training for these races left their mark even on one-off participants - and for many opened the door to a fitter and healthier lifestyle. It became fashionable to become fit, an image that was pushed (and still is) by sports equipment manufacturers and the marketing men of the food producers.

It was a circus for the people, but the marathons did inspire many potatoes to get off the couch, the two main reasons being the constant media hype and the ease with which you could get started - you just bought a pair of trainers and hit the tarmac, without being stared at or considered mad - or at least your madness was accepted.

It is still a very available way of exercising - canal tow paths, public parks and quiet streets are readily available to the vast majority and it is easy for the committed to squeeze in a lunch-time run or jog.

It is good exercise, particularly for the legs and the old cardiovascular, but the down side seems to be the amount of injuries to which runners are prone and the number of runners that succumb to them. As with a lot of sports, the principal cause of injury is the participant themselves - injuries occur through over-training, by not seeking medical help when injuries do occur, by ignoring pain and other symptoms and by re-embarking on training programmes prior to full recovery.

The knee and ankle joints and their associated tendons, muscles and ligaments are the main areas of weakness and most prone to damage. After this it's the lower back and hips. Prevention here is definitely preferable to cure, and the first step, no pun intended, is to buy a good pair of proper running shoes. Today's running shoes look like props from old "Flash Gordon" movies, and if you believe the manufacturer's blurb, the only reason mankind lasted this long without them is due to the grace of God. The bottom line is that you're looking for a shoe that fits properly - ie. one that supports your foot and heel without putting pressure on your Achilles tendon, and a shoe that will absorb as much of the eight tons or so of impact that you place on your joints every time you put your heel down.

Another way to help avoid injury, and save your run to boot, is to avoid training on tarmac or hard surfaces too often, and help your ankles by being very careful on irregular surfaces. So, its off for a run round the park for you. Watch the kerb.

As with any form of exercise, eat properly, sleep lots, warm up, stretch, warm down, don't over-train, don't expect miracles, and research your training programme carefully.

Swimming
Reckoned by those that know (fish) to be the best all-round exercise on the go. It is very gentle on the joints because your weight is borne by the water, and unless you bump into the end of the pool, is free from impact and shock loading. Every muscle group is used and gently stretched, although cramp can be a problem, and like every form of exercise you really should do some stretching before you enter the Big Blue and play at Great Whites. It is also very accessible and is a very convenient lunch-hour exercise. Those whom I've talked to who are really into swimming talk about the therapeutic feeling that swimming endless lengths gives them. Living in the west coast of Scotland, I feel I spend enough of my time soaked to the skin and like many people I find it a very boring pastime, but an excellent way to keep fit.

They say that swimming is like riding a bike. I think the comparison is based on the fact that it's a skill developed by the left-hand side of your brain rather than anything else. Personally, I've never seen a bicycle in my local pool, but I, like many, swim with the same style, panache and efficiency as I did when I first imitated a cork as opposed to a brick at around the age of eight years old. All pools offer some kind of lessons and there is no harm and a lot to be gained from having a professional give a few tips to help you improve - even if you are a good swimmer. Do it tomorrow - support your local pool - after all, as a taxpayer you have shares in it.

Swimming can also be a very sociable activity, one that all the family can join in with. It can also be a very anti-social activity, as most pools open early in the morning during the week to allow you to take some exercise before going to work. So you arrive in the office feeling fit, looking good and obnoxiously cheery...

Squash/tennis/racquet ball/football/hockey etc.

These are good sports for all-round fitness provided you are working at your aerobic training level, which doesn't seem to be a problem. They are very good for toning up muscles and agility. They are very good at hurting you too. Rapid acceleration, deceleration and changes of direction place terrible strains and impacts on your body, namely your legs and heels, as in running. Unlike running this kind of activity also has a high proportion of lateral strain too, putting the ligaments, tendons and cartilages of the ankles and knees under a lot of pressure. I'm being very objective about this because those who enthuse about these sports are generally well aware of the risks involved, and choose to participate because the pleasures outweigh those possible risks. And choice is what freedom's all about, so go for it.

However, an occasional player shouldn't view a sudden increase in participation as a quick route to fitness. More likely a quick route to the sports injuries clinic. Also, a few games of squash, etc per week is probably not enough to get you trek fit and will need to be supplemented with a programme designed to attack your weak areas. Whether you participate to complete, to relax or to add to your keep fit programme don't forget it's doing you good and creating a healthy routine.

MENTAL EXERCISE

If it takes three men two days to dig a hole.... Everyone now knows the value of physical exercise and how important it is to the success of a trek, but have you considered how important mental preparation is? And as it's possible to improve your stamina and strength through physical exercise, so is it possible to become stronger mentally by doing a few inner exercises to increase your patience, tolerance and level of motivation. Believe me, if you are going to be travelling far, or are organising your own trip, then you'll need to be pretty relaxed or you'll fail. Don't forget - this is meant to be a holiday. You are not going to see or enjoy much if you are not relaxed. Just as for physical fitness, mental fitness is not going to happen overnight or without effort - it takes dedication, commitment and perseverance. Now, just as I feel the cynics about to turn to the next chapter I want to make some things clear. This is not just some Hippy Cosmic Inner Pseudo Psycho New Wave Self Analysis born of too many years in Asia and funny cigarettes. It's the observations of many trekkers and mountaineers. Many people fail on trek, and on climbs, because they don't have the mental strength to help see them through discomfort and drive them on to succeed. They can't relax enough to project beyond what they haven't got, to appreciate what they do have, or have the mental agility to avoid letting minor physical ailments dominate their thoughts and attitude. Success in the mountains is more often due to strength in the head rather than the legs.

Here is how it's done. You learn to relax. How is up to you, whether it is through yoga, meditation, self-hypnosis or whatever. Your GP will be able to give you some help in this department if you need it. You then learn to sneak in relaxation sessions during the day - not major lying-on-the-office-floor-in-a-trance stuff but a 15 minute read of a trash novel during tea break, a slow floppy lunch time run, or 20 minutes sitting alone at the back of a church. Become aware of when you are becoming tense and talk yourself out of it. Imagine a devil on one shoulder, the angel on the other - it's the devil that's winding you up, so dismiss him and listen to what the angel has to say. Look at other people and learn from them - "doesn't Smith look ridiculous when he's wound up. I'm above and beyond that kind of pitiful behaviour and will not let myself look like him in front of my peers.... Jones is a very together person who does not panic, remains calm and gets respect and the job done. I can be as cool as her."

If you don't like what's going on around you, switch off and go somewhere else. Long uphill grinds are my trigger to switch off and think about re-building my car gearbox or work out how the stripe gets into toothpaste or how many packets of jelly one would need to buy to fill an average size swimming pool. If your imagination is lacking try carrying a copy of *The Cremation of Sam McGee* by Robert Service around with you to memorise, and impress your fellow directors/workers/trekkers by reciting this humorous ballad to them after three weeks of holiday.

Of course, we all reach the stage of wanting to punch the next person to say "there's always somebody worse off than you," because there isn't. In which case you burst into tears. And then you'll feel a lot better. I only want to make you aware of the need for mental preparation, and these are a few guide-lines. Like physical preparation, it's up to you to design your own programme. The benefits cannot be over-stressed. Stress? Who mentioned stress....

The Runners Handbook: The Classic Fitness Guide for Beginning and Intermediate Runners by Bob Glover and Jack Shepard (Penguin books)
Your Personal Trainer - General Fitness Guide by Anne Goodsell (Boxtree Publishing, Broadwall House, 21 Broadwall, London SE1 9PL)
Training for Peak Performance by Wilf Paish (Black Publishing)
The English YMCA Guide to Exercise to Music by Rodney Cullum and Lesley Mowbray (Pelham Books)
Taking the Plunge - Swimming for Fitness by Penny Clarke (Boxtree Publishing)
The book of Soft Martial Arts (Chi Kung, Pa Kua and T'ai Chi) (Gai Books)

A useful phone number: YMCA Fitness Advice Bureau (01800) 808089

IMMUNISATION
Even the fittest body and the healthiest attitude cannot create an immunity, or aid recovery, when faced with the world-prevalent diseases. This is the big league of the world's killers: tetanus, polio, typhoid etc, all easily avoided by immunisation, for us at least, but sadly a way of life, and death, for so many people in the Third and Developing Worlds.

The following is a good guide on what to take for where. Check with the Department of Health (address at the end) for an up-to-date report on your particular destination, and to confirm if there are any changes to this information. Either make direct contact with the department or ask your high street travel agent to check with "Prestel" on their computer.

Most vaccines do not come under the umbrella of National Health Service cover, and will have to be paid for privately. Pharmacists are unlikely to carry stocks of most vaccines, so it is probable that they will have to be ordered, although most can be obtained within 24 hours. Whilst paying for this service, and it can be as much as £30.00 for a single vaccine, insist on a vaccination certificate: a) so that you know when to renew it and b) to keep immigration officers sweet by offering evidence of your vaccinations. Certifying each vaccination eliminates any doubts as to whether a certificate is necessary - overkill maybe. This year, who knows what any particular nation will demand prior to entry next season. And as stated earlier, these will serve as a personal reminder.

Vaccines are made up of inactivated or modified live "bugs" or their products. Most vaccines produce their protective effect by stimulating the production of antibodies or antitoxins. Following a full course of these antibody or antitoxin levels remain high for months or years, thus providing a good level of protection against infection until a booster is due. The effects of being vaccinated with typhoid, yellow fever or whatever is, for some people, barely discernible. Others, myself included, drop like drugged rhinos and are bedridden for days after. Most people are some way in between, but allow time for this process to take its course before going on your travels. Children under nine months and pregnant women should not be immunised - consult your GP if in doubt.

Descriptions of the worst offenders are detailed in Chapter Five, but here is a rundown of what precautions should be taken for where.

EASTERN - CENTRAL EUROPE
Diphtheria, hepatitis A, polio, mild typhoid, rabies

ASIA AND THE FAR EAST
Tetanus, polio, hepatitis A, typhoid, meningitis (A + C - India and Nepal),

malaria prophylaxis, rabies, Japanese encephalitis

MIDDLE EAST
Tetanus, polio, hepatitis A, typhoid, meningitis (A + C - Saudi Arabia), malaria prophylaxis, rabies

NORTH AFRICA
Tetanus, polio, hepatitis A, typhoid, malaria prophylaxis, rabies

TROPICAL AFRICA AND TROPICAL SOUTH AMERICA
Tetanus, polio, hepatitis A, typhoid, yellow fever, meningitis (A + C), malaria prophylaxis
   Other vaccines may be recommended depending on whether the area you are travelling through or to is currently infected.

Rabies
As rabies is a viral infection (like Aids), prevention by means of vaccination does not have a great reputation for success, and is a particularly nasty jab to receive. Even if immunised against rabies, it does not remove the need to have immediate medical attention should you be bitten by an infected beasty, so immunisation is really only recommended to those likely to be away from medical help or travelling through remote areas, like trekkers.

Cholera
An infection on the increase, this can easily be avoided by sterilising all water and maintaining high standards of hygiene. A vaccine of dubious effectiveness is available to those travellers who will be spending time in high risk areas - usually overlanders who travel from area to area relatively quickly.

Japanese encephalitis
Another viral infection, most prominent in South East Asia and prevalent during the monsoon. A vaccine is recommended for visitors likely to be staying for more than one month.

USEFUL ADDRESSES
Department of Health Helpline (will send appropriate literature free) (0800) 555 777

The Thomas Cook Travel Clinic
45, Barclay Street
Piccadilly, London W1A 1ES
(0171) 499 4000
Open 8:30-3:30 Monday to Friday, Saturday by appointment.
   Immunisation service plus shop with associated goods - mosquito nets, first-aid kits etc.

CHAPTER FIVE
On trek health

"The art of medicine consists of amusing the patient while Nature cures the disease." Voltaire

Welcome to the biggest section of the book, and if size is any indication of importance, welcome to a very important section of the book. And yes, you are allowed to read this before you go on trek.

PAYING FOR MEDICAL CARE
As members of the EC we have reciprocal rights to medical treatment on the produciton of a UK passport and a form E111 (available from your local Post Office, Travel Agent or DSS office) and a wad of cash, monies spent being reimbursed by means of a rather complicated process. All this is explained in the Department of Health's excellent little leaflet *Health Advice For Travellers* available at the above outlets. It is important to make sure that your E111 is stamped by the Post Office.

Outside the EC insurance is needed, and with the exception of the UK any rescue must be paid for. Apart from which, insurance allows a choice, where it exists, as to where you are treated, and by whom.

Even if one is insured, it is usually necessary to pay up front for treatment and funds are reimbursed later by the insurers on delivery of receipts - see under "Insurance". So, even if travelling close to home, be fully insured prior to departure.

Finding a doctor on trek can be hard; you may have to play at being doctor for yourself - or others. Hopefully, none of the advice being offered will be needed, and should it be, then it will help to make your homecoming as cheery as the start of your trek. If nothing else, I hope this section helps you to appreciate what can go wrong if you're not alert or prepared. Winter hill-walkers carry (or should) a phenomenal amount of equipment on their snowy sojourns - 90 per cent of it never being used. But it is always carried. It is like a talisman, and by continuing to carry it, it will, hopefully, never be needed.

When I throw my rucksack over my shoulder and set off to the winter hills I don't say "My God, I hope I won't have to use that bivi bag/first-aid kit/ emergency food/spare gloves!" Rather than being stressed by what's in my rucksack I'm comforted by it. Take comfort in these pages. It's like first-aid,

A Pakistani porter crossing a stream *(Author)*

A pleasant walk through a valley in the Tien Shan range, Kazakhstan.
Walking poles are becoming increasingly popular *(Author)*

A high camp in the Hungu Valley, Nepal *(Author)*
The Horombo Hut on the popular Kilimanjaro trek *(W. Unsworth)*

something you learn, update and practise, not because every day in life presents an unfortunate opportunity to use it, but because one day there may be a situation in which these skills and knowledge are needed. View the following in the same way.

If you can't see the simile because you are not a first-aider then become a first-aider before going on trek. I haven't included first-aid in this book other than in relation to specific quirks of trekking, eg. blisters. But it is in your own interests and those of your group that you should be armed with the basics - it's no good leaving it to the trek doctor or leader to sort things out. As human beings they may need assistance, may not be there, or could be the casualty. (See *First Aid for Hillwalkers* by Renouf and Hulse, Cicerone)

If the following section was expanded to include every ailment known to have hit trekkers, then the day after publication by Murphy's Law some poor trekker would go down with a disease thought only to affect Amazonian parrots. It is simply a guide to the most common and potentially dangerous health hazards trekkers face, so please be aware that this is not definitive.

I've tried to keep the physiology simple, mentioning it only where it is relevant to treatment, to try and make clear the reasons behind the sometimes rather strange courses of action. I am neither a physician nor a pharmacist nor a physiologist. You would never have guessed, would you?

I am deeply saddened when I witness trekkers with diarrhoea - it is a most depressing, debilitating, not to say embarrassing affliction. Unlike a cut, a bruise or sunburn, there is no detracting from it - it is omnipresent and try as one might, the mind cannot be persuaded to be side-tracked from wondering when it will all end.

I am angered when I hear trekkers and travellers bragging about having Giardia or dysentery. In the cafes and bars of the tourist areas there is a sub-culture that views lost pounds as a measure of experience; a skeletal frame is physical testimony to their epic trip and a mark of their tenacity. However, given that in some trekking areas there is a 50 per cent infant mortality rate, this attitude is an insult to the host country. Diarrhoea happens, and some of the bugs picked up during a trek seem immortal; when you've been hit by one, there is a story to tell, and it's often humour that lifts us out of these black times. But if you've walked through Trekland with your eyes open, you'll realise what real misery uncontrolled dysentery brings, and you won't brag about yours...

Maintaining good health on trek is of paramount importance and is easily achieved provided the trekker stays aware of the problems and does not become complacent. Regardless of where you are, whether it be in the heat, the cold or up high, polluted water is the prime enemy, but when cleaned becomes your best friend. So without much ado let's take the plunge.

WATER

Water gives the body a reservoir to help fight illness, fatigue, the effects of heat, altitude and cold. In all trekking situations it should be drunk constantly, little but often. Your metabolism and circumstances will dictate the amount, but 4 litres of water daily, or about half a litre of water for each 5 degrees centigrade of heat, plus as much tea, juice or other non-alcoholic fluids as you think you can manage, is a fair guide. In addition to this you'll need clean water for brushing your teeth, washing your delicate bits and any minor cuts and grazes you may collect during your day. The yard-stick by which to measure your fluid intake is to watch your urine levels. Urine should be clear and copious. Any colour in there, or only a couple of wees a day means that you are not drinking enough. This is known as the "Golden Rule": clear and copious.

Establishing a source of clean water in camp is a first priority, and a simple system for producing this must be established before trekking starts. If a system is in operation from the onset then trekkers and crew will fall into a comfortable routine as to how water is cleaned, and where in camp it will be found. To ensure daily consistency, it is best that one person (on a commercial trip the trek leader) be made responsible for this. Whether the job is delegated on a day-to-day basis is then left up to that one person, but the job still remains their responsibility, thus ensuring it is done, and with consistency. Rotas, apart from smacking of the workplace, fall apart too easily, especially as this is a holiday.

Twenty litre plastic Jerry cans, with taps in the bottom, are ideal; for a group of ten, three will suffice. Keep one in the cook tent, one in the mess tent and one in reserve. If 60 litres seems like a lot of water it's not - a group of ten will empty one can at breakfast just by filling up their water bottles. Always draw water from upstream of camp, even if it is to be cleaned.

It is a common myth that by residing in a country long enough one can wean oneself onto drinking the local water. It is just that, a myth; for every strong healthy native who thrives on the local aqua vitae there is one with constant diarrhoea, and many who never made it to adulthood but were killed by the water before they could speak their first words.

There are three methods of cleansing water - boiling, chemical and mechanical.

Boiling

When water boils at sea level, 100°C (212°F), the temperature is sufficient to kill most bacteria, to eliminate bacterial spores however requires a constant temperature of 160°C for 10 minutes. It is impossible to achieve this temperature on a camp stove, and in addition water boils at significantly lower temperatures at altitude, where even 100°C is unobtainable. In addition boiling water is very time-consuming and for the amounts required by the average group is a real bind on fuel, and the resources in the kitchen. It also creates a demand on the forests of the world which struggle to serve the local needs, never mind a group of trekkers and their crew. Using firewood is definitely unecological and even the alternative fuels are questionable due to the amounts required, so boiling, whilst good in an emergency, is far from ideal, leaving chemical and mechanical means the only really practical alternatives.

Chemical

There are various means of chemically cleaning water. By far the most popular is the use of purification tablets, either chlorine or iodine based. As iodine kills a far broader range of bacteria than chlorine, the latter has become unpopular of late, and iodine based tablets are the norm and should be the trekker's first choice. Implementation couldn't be easier, the tablets being dissolved in the appropriate amount of water as per instructions. Most tablets sterilise one litre of water and require 30 minutes to do what sterilising tablets do. Jumbo tablets are available, not for sterilising elephants but for cleaning 20-25 litres at a time, essential for big groups or expeditions. (Also essential is a big container to keep it in.) The down side is the taste, easily masked by tea, or fruit juice additives, or given time, ignored.

Closely related to this is tincture of iodine. Dropped into water at a strength of 1:8,000,000 (or something like that) iodine needs 20 minutes to clean. If, like me, you are not a chemist, try using an eye dropper to drop four drops per litre into low risk water (good hotels, etc.) or seven into water of unknown source. As was stated earlier, allow at least 20 minutes (30, if water is cold) for it to work.

Tincture of iodine is readily available throughout the world and is a quick and effective method of cleaning water. Carried easily in a small bottle it does not go out of date, or break up and turn to dust as does its close relative, the purification tablet. Whether used daily or not, it should be carried as an emergency back-up. It comes in various strengths - 2 per cent being adequate for most situations and the basis of the aforementioned proportions. The official line is not to carry iodine in anything other than glass bottles. Although I cannot recommend this, I know several people who have carried it in heavy polythene bottles for considerable times without any adverse effect.

Iodine will gather in the thyroid gland, any excess being flushed out via the body's fluids. Breast feeding mothers should therefore avoid prolonged use, or high levels, of iodine as the effects of high concentrations of it in children are largely unknown. Another way in which iodine is used is in crystal form. A concentrate is made up by adding a small amount of water to crystals of iodine contained by a mesh within a bottle, which also acts as a measure. The concentrate is then used in a similar fashion to tincture of iodine. Measured bottles containing iodine crystals as described are available commercially. If it doesn't appeal, or you are one of the very few people allergic to iodine, then there is only one option left -

Mechanical water treatment

Not as fearsome as it sounds, mechanical water treatment basically involves pumping water through a very fine filter. By very fine we are talking about 4 to 2 microns; any bigger than this may not stop the arch-enemy, Giardia, from getting into the water. Flushing water through something this fine is a slow and hard process but the end result is chemical and bacteria free with no taint of other obnoxious substances. However, viruses and strong chemical pollutants can slip through and will need strong chemicals to sort them out. The incredibly small pore-size of these filters makes them expensive to produce and leaves them prone to clogging up very quickly, particularly in the case of glacial meltwater. The better filters will have an integral cleaning system, or a series of internal mesh filters, or both as a way of preventing the main core filter blocking. For the trekker who's going to be away from home for more than three months this is the ideal system, but even the small filters are expensive, and for a large group the cost of having enough filters to provide the volume of water required is almost prohibitive. Even the robust need careful looking after and a comprehensive stock of spares and lubricants should be carried with them.

GASTRO-INTESTINAL PROBLEMS - PREVENTION

Personal and camp hygiene are the next line of defence after clean water. High standards are very easy to establish but one must be vigilant to maintain them. Hard as it is to do so, try and keep nails and hands clean at all times - we all put our hands to our mouth at some stage of the day. Next keep your body as clean as you can, especially round one's little private orifices - potential breeding ground for all sorts of nasties. The key to this is either keeping a small sponge or flannel in the top of your rucksack alongside a small bar of soap - as found in hotels. The water comes from your bottle - poured onto the cloth, don't let it touch the neck of the bottle. Baby bottom wipes are very handy, but can dry out leaving you with a rather rough and useless bit of tissue. Even those that are foil sealed, as supplied by airlines, are prone to this. Having said that, take some with you because they are luxurious and very refreshing!

Prevention - food/cross-infection

Preparation of food and water is to gastro-intestinal disorders what acclimatisation is to altitude. Backed up by responsible garbage and toilet

Lovely to look at, but carriers of so many nasties

procedures, those bugs are going to have to work very hard to get into your insides. As with any ailment, prevention is better than cure, but even the most vigilant can let the odd bug through the net and succumb to the "Katmandu Quick-Step" or whatever. Unless you can personally vouch that meals have been prepared properly then you should avoid any salad, sliced tomatoes or onions. Fruit salads, fresh fruit juices and ice-cream are also on the hit list, and if you think you'll pass on the food and just have a drink instead then pass on the ice and insist that any soft drinks are opened in front of you. A common scam is to dilute soft drinks with tap and mineral water, making four bottles out of three. Hot food is generally okay as small restaurants tend only to cook on demand, and it is the bigger hotels and restaurants that are likely to have the big hot plates where buffet meals will lie tepid for a couple of hours or so.

Salad and fruit are not out altogether - they just need to be prepared. Salads should have been soaked in iodine or potassium permanganate for 20 minutes, and with any other food - boil it, bake it, peel it or forget it. See, you do need that knife. Hot drinks tend to get boiled and most are okay. It is a gamble though. In squalid up-country shacks you are on guard but often it's the up-market hotels that catch you offguard - the kitchens often fall short of the standards maintained in luxurious lounges and bedrooms. Our society latched onto the ideas of hygiene about the mid 19th century and it's taken us about 150 years to reach the standards of hygiene we maintain now - can you honestly expect another culture to absorb the principals overnight? I should think not.

I suspect almost everyone has some kind of stomach bug when they first arrive in Trekland. Coming from our sterile society our stomachs have a bit of adjusting to do, like developing a whole load of new enzymes to help with the old digestion. Add a few days of travel, jet lag, apprehension, a lack of sleep and the heat and it's no surprise that for a few days most people suffer from "Flying Tummy" and as long as it's only a few days and not completely out of control then let it take its course and have Mother Nature rearm you.

This is usually the time when you are in the capital getting in supplies and waiting for permits, so you can afford that luxury.

Once you start on trek it becomes a bit more than just an inconvenience to keep on allowing nature to sort it out. On trek there is already a risk of dehydration and having a digestive system that can't keep a grip on the fluids and food that you are taking in is going to leave you weak and dried out. Not a very good start. Apart from that there is also the very genuine risk of cross-infection. Once on trek people tend to live in quite close proximity to each other, sharing communal utensils. After a couple of days of being ill, the chance of them infecting another with the same thing is quite high, I'd say about 80 per cent. So despite your gut feelings (sorry) at that stage it's time to start chemical warfare and break open the drugs box. Any earlier than after a couple of days is possibly too early, by not allowing the body to adapt to its new surroundings.

Cross-infection is hard to prevent and necessitates a well organised camp. Beside the latrine and outside the mess tent there should be a jug of mild disinfectant to wash hands after going to the loo and before dining. Each individual should pour the water over their own hands and then discard - a communal bowl of water quickly becomes a germ soup. Use personal towels or air dry hands - shared towels are a potential source of cross-infection. Never offer, or take, a drink from someone else's water bottle; and as our mouths are in contact with our mugs everyone should have their own personal one. Names can be marked on direct with felt pen (removed at end of trek with Meths) or by a zinc-oxide tape label, again removable at the end of the trek.

Stainless steel cutlery and crockery is the most hygienic. Plastic, regardless of quality, scratches, leaving a trough to trap infection. Stainless can also be boiled, not at all a bad thing. Should there be an infection in camp then all the crockery and cutlery should be sterilised after each meal by washing in a hot antiseptic solution. It needn't be so strong as to leave a taste. Dry in the air or with clean cloths. Ensure that the support crew have their own mugs too; what's sauce for the sahib is sauce for the cook, after all. It's no use presuming that the crew are preparing food and maintaining hygiene properly, it must be monitored constantly, albeit discretely. Grabbing a quick brew with the boys in the cook tent is usually welcomed and offers a quick sneak at how things are looking. Don't be shy about rolling up your sleeves and getting stuck in yourself - show the crew the standards you expect them to maintain and how to achieve them.

Garbage disposal

Our rubbish and waste is the potential source of unnecessary disease and infection. At best, leaving rubbish and waste around is an act of gross irresponsibility, but more often should be viewed as a criminal act which it would be in this country. From a purely health point of view disposal of rubbish and waste on trek must be given the same care and attention as any other aspect of camp hygiene. It is often the most neglected area because it's an unpleasant task and embarrassing to talk about. Sadly, it is not always the trekker who becomes ill either; our mess becomes a legacy that our hosts inherit.

In the ideal world everything that was packed in on a trek would be packed out - a rule in all the US National Parks - but the reality is somewhat different. Certainly the better commercial operators are leading the way by carrying out as much garbage as is possible. The real problem is the cost of hiring extra porters and one created by the tradition of the local cultures. Organic waste has traditionally been turned back into the soil, and nothing else was thrown away...and then in come the trekkers with tin-cans, batteries, polythene bags, sanitary towels and toilet paper. In many cultures villages and porters are quite happy to have our garbage dumped in their village, and on the trail; small children and animals view it as a treasure trove and rummage through it to see what turns up. Villages accept our rubbish as a by-product, the income trekkers provide overriding any objections.

Our medieval towns were, by and large, dung heaps with animal and human waste lying around in the streets, and there are vast areas in the developing world where this is still the case. That doesn't give us the right to do like-wise; if we do then we've made no progress since our medieval ancestors and shouldn't be allowed out of the shire! I certainly know of areas in Pakistan and Nepal where villagers and Sirdars have become very tuned in to what makes trekkers happy (neat and tidy villages and trails) and have organised dumps and public toilets to facilitate this, and will chastise messy groups. The concept of public health hasn't quite been realised, but as an offshoot of cleaning up, the message is beginning to filter through. Some friends and myself have tried to carry out all our rubbish only to have bewildered porters lighten their loads by dumping most of it as soon as our backs were turned. But we'll keep trying and would encourage others to do so. Please.

Garbage

If garbage has to be dumped then do so in a responsible manner. Here are a few guidelines. First, does it need to go up country in the first place? Imported goods tend to be double and triple wrapped. Some of that wrapping can be left behind. Can it be recycled? Either by you or the crew? Glass screwtop jars and good polythene containers are useful throughout the world! Anything else? If unwanted, is it degradeable? A paper bag or potato peelings dug into the soil or deep in the compost heap will biodegrade. But will that polythene bag, if not degrade, at least break down? Think before dumping.

Glass, thrown into fast moving glacial rivers, will be ground to dust very quickly. Tin cans, burned to break the tin coating, then crushed will rust to dust, if buried. Polythene can be burned, as can paper, at the price of releasing more pollutants and heat into the atmosphere. Unpleasant as this is, I find it easier to live with than the thought that a child somewhere is seriously ill through an infection that my old can has caused, or a villager's valuable cow has died from eating an old polythene bag. Aluminium, of course can be recycled, but not up country. As a compromise, instead of trying to bring all your garbage back, just return with the stuff that cannot be disposed of in a satisfactory manner up country.

Rubbish pits should be damp and deep and at least 100m away from any water source. Big raging rivers tend not to be used for local water supplies - they often contain too much silt and local streams are slower, clearer and more accessible. Bear this in mind when pitching camp and digging holes. Keep the first tuft of any hole as the lid. When the hole is finished with try and drop a big boulder down first - one that scavenging animals and small children cannot move. Fill in the hole then replace turf. I know of one Sirdar who buried some rubbish under a main trail - his reasoning being that countless feet packed down the soil, quickly disguising the site and preventing it from being re-excavated. A good point I suppose.

Deep crevasses are another popular dump with the added advantage of having the weight of a glacier to bear down on the rubbish grinding it to nothing... I hope. The dangerous part is dumping it there in the first place. However, if woolly mammoths and expired mountaineers come out of glaciers recognisable after centuries, how much of our rubbish will do the same? And will the archaeologists be pleased or appalled? Dead batteries must come home to be disposed of, although most now contain no mercury.

Be one step ahead and plan your rubbish. Have it degradable or better still recyclable, be an eco-trekker and keep your camp healthy.

Toilets
Is there a portable toilet out there that is in any way practical for a trekking group? Something like a portable dry vented system that could be emptied daily in the local dung heap, with perhaps an organic additive to render the contents safe and break down into useful manure? If anybody knows of one please let me know! Groups are bad news because they create a lot of waste in a small space; individuals are easier to cope with. Let's start with the individual or small group.

Westerners create two problems when they go to the loo: 1) the stools, 2) the loo roll. Being shy creatures, we all tend to hide when we need to go - a shady spot, hidden from view, where the sun don't shine - the worst place from an ecological point of view. Defecation in the open is what's needed, then the sun can dry it, and in an estimated four days it'll have turned to dust and be gone. Especially if you spread it about. Seriously! Dung spread out over a rock will either dry out or wash into the soil very quickly. If you are in a damp moist place then burying it will help it to rot down quickly - so you'll need a small trowel with you. Remember to keep downstream of your water supply, and a hundred metres from the river unless you are near one of those big fast-flowing rivers mentioned earlier. Defecating in the river isn't possible, but urinating is - dilution being the solution to pollution, but not into the local water supply. Spread it about or bury it deep. Covering it with rocks does nothing but preserve it for someone to stand on, or worse...

Toilet Paper
Toilet paper. What do people think happens to the reams of toilet paper that they leave lying around? Is this some animalistic territory-making ritual? Am I stupid, or over-reacting, or is leaving used toilet paper lying around in someone else's countryside one of the most ignorant, inconsiderate, potentially harmful, thoughtless acts that we, as trekkers, commit?

The solution is quick and simple - carry a cigarette lighter with you when you go to the loo - spread out your used paper and burn it. It's sanitary and effective. Sanitary towels and disposable nappies require care in their disposal. If buried en route to camp then they need to be buried deep to prevent being excavated by keen snouted animals. By far the best method is incineration, but this requires a pretty big fire. The compromise is to put them down the toilet pit. Thankfully biodegradable nappies are quite common now, unlike the first generation models which are reckoned to have a 500 year half life....

Groups present more of a problem because of the amount of people concentrated in a small area and groups tend to use the same sites. Apart from the superloo sought after in the first paragraph the most popular and practical method of relieving the masses seems to be a large hole in the ground. Dig it deep, dig it narrow. For the sake of modesty erect a little loo tent over the hole. Ask people to burn their paper down the hole and to finish their business by throwing in a handful of earth, as a substitute for flushing. Loo tents don't need to be big, but they do need to be robust - zips tend to die and a tie door is a much more practical option. The interior is kept simple - a string holding the loo roll, and long, flat stones to place the feet on. Forget about seating - these get mucked up (unhealthy) and encourage users to stay too long! Besides, squatting is far better for you.... Don't forget the jug of washing water beside the door. If you really want to make your tent luxurious then wrap some bicycle handle bar tape to the two forward upright poles of the tent... For a rest day, or at a standing camp, several sites will need to be prepared. Don't wait until the old one is full before digging its successor. Don't dig the successor in line between the old hole and the mess tent, or people will find it in the night. And don't let the hole fill up with excrement. Stop a foot from the rim, throw in the basin of disinfected water and fill it up with soil. Finish off with that turf lid. This system has its critics, but apart from digging and lining a vented toilet - basically a huge pit with an enclosed top and narrow deposit slit - I can't think of a better one. I suspect that the little house on the prairie is unpopular because it's not a macho piece of mountaineering kit, or because they tend to be a little bit wee.

Above the snow-line brings its own problems. Faeces buried in the snow tend to reappear when the snow contracts, creating a health hazard and ruining the environment. The only solution is to take it down. Use the trowel as a poop-scoop and collect the business in a poly bag. Once down below the snow-line it can be buried as before. A toilet site can be created using snowblocks, with a fixed rope leading to it for night-time sorties.

Digging and cleaning up the toilet site should be the personal responsibility of the Trek Leader. It pushes to the limits of what the service crew can really be expected to do. It is an odious task but a necessary one. There is a fun side to it though - with imagination the loo tent can be pitched in some fantastic locations with stunning views and for sure you'll get half an hour's solitude when you're digging that hole. And completely ignored when tidying it up!

Food, water, toilet and rubbish - the four horsemen of the tummy bug. But as has already been stated, accidents can happen so let's have a look at some of the possibilities.

One last word though - soft quilted toilet rolls and wet wipes can exchange hands for many dollars two weeks into trek...after a month single sheets become currency.

GASTRO-INTESTINAL TROUBLES - TREATMENT

If prevention hasn't worked then don't lie down on the track, waiting for the vultures; all is certainly not lost. Most forms of diarrhoea will pass (I do apologise) as the body works out the cut of the villain within and learns to fight it. Apart from the inconvenience of having to dive into the bushes, often in mid-sentence, the most bothersome bit is trying to pore in enough fluid to prevent dehydration. At the first sign of loose stools reach for the Oral Rehydration Salts (ORS). Follow the instructions carefully and drink, drink, drink. In spite of having diarrhoea you should still be urinating clear and copious.

It is dehydration that kills babies in the Third World, not diarrhoea itself. If it's no go, before reaching for the Anti-Bs try a milder alternative, like Diocalm. We tend to take antibiotics for granted here in the west, and don't really appreciate what an impact they can have on our bodies. It's best to try, for a few days at least, to let our bodies cope with things by themselves.

Antibiotics

There is a temptation to start taking antibiotics at the immediate onset of any kind of bowel irregularity. This is not advisable, however, as it may take two days to assess what kind of bug one has, and the course of antibiotics appropriate to cure it. Prolonged or inappropriate use of antibiotics can also have the opposite of the desired effect, and actually cause loose stools. Antibiotics tend to be indiscriminate when they clean up the intestinal jungle; no prisoners are taken and they wipe out the good as well as the bad guys. It can take a while for the good guys to re-establish themselves, so they can leave one feeling a bit weak and a bit vulnerable. Antibiotics also tend to lower one's resistance to UV light, so take even more care in the sun.

For the ladies it's even worse news. Strong antibiotics often, though not always, are responsible for vaginal thrush - just what you want on the Patagonia ice-cap - and can seriously weaken or cancel out the effects of the contraceptive pill. As of course so can sickness and diarrhoea...ask my sister. Better still, ask my nephew. My brother-in-law recommends that alternative methods of contraception should be considered. So before you break out the antibiotics try something milder like Diocalm and whatever you do, don't wear braces on your trousers.

Bowel Paralyzers

These are drugs which will stop diarrhoea and give one relief from relieving one's self. However, as the whole purpose of diarrhoea is to flush out toxins and give the body a chance to recuperate, these drugs can be quite dangerous in that they relieve the symptoms but don't eliminate the cause. By retaining toxins in our tums we grant them the perfect breeding ground. They should therefore only be used when taking antibiotics. Apart from the feeling of confidence they offer, BPs also do allow one to pour in a lot of liquid. And we all know how important that is.... The two most commonly available are Lomotil and Imodium (2mg). The dose for Lomotil is four tablets initially followed by two tablets six hourly until the diarrhoea is controlled. The dose for Imodium is two capsules initially followed by one capsule after each loose stool to a maximum of 16mg daily. NEVER ADMINISTER THESE DRUGS TO CHILDREN, they can have lethal results. Hated by doctors, with good reasons, BPs can be justified - queuing at airports and long bus journeys to name but two. But please, if you are going to use these, be sensible and only use them as necessary.

It must be stated again that the advice and information offered here is no substitute for that from a physician and is only to be considered if the world is falling out your bottom and medical advice and care are not available. There is no known medical cure for viral infections and no real way of diagnosing them outside a medical laboratory.

If you have suffered something nasty on trek then it is advisable to have tests done on your return just to ensure that you aren't playing host to some dormant exotic visitor, ie. worms. It is not unknown for "Trekker's Tum" to re-appear long after you have forgotten those bad times on trek.

Food poisoning
Symptoms

Explosive, smelly, watery diarrhoea and vomiting (or nausea) one to six hours after eating. Settles very quickly after food has been evacuated and unlikely to last more than five or six hours - probably food poisoning if other people in the party are struck simultaneously. May be accompanied by short-lived, though severe, stomach cramps.

Treatment

If symptoms as above then no action other than bland foods, lots of fluids and ORS.

Bacterial dysentery
Symptoms

Watery stools (frequent), abdominal cramps, mild fever, nausea and very occasionally, vomiting. The diarrhoea is sudden in its onset and occasionally the stools contain some blood. 2-10 day duration.

Treatment

Ciprofloxacin (Ciproxin) 250mg. 1 tab 4 times daily for 5 days.

Alternatively, Trimethoprim 200mg. 1 tab 2 times daily for 5 days.

Ciproxin should be taken two hours after eating. Do not mix with indigestion remedies or alcohol.

Amoebic dysentery
The least common but most serious of the trekker's diarrhoeas.
Symptoms
Frequent bowel movements with small amounts of stool, painful stomach cramps which abate to omnipresent but mild abdominal pain. Stools can become mucousy and bloody. This condition can be very fatiguing with accompanying irritability and occasionally nervousness. Pain (mild) may occur in the muscles, back or joints, accompanied by mild fever. Weight loss may be expected.
Treatment
Metronidazole (Flagyl) 400mg. 2 tabs 3 times daily for 5-10 days **or** Tinidazole (Fasigyn) 500mg. 4 tabs 1 time daily for 2-3 days.
Fasigyn leaves a nasty metallic taste in the mouth so, if possible, take in the evening and sleep away the taste. The large dose may also cause nausea. Alcohol should not be taken with either drugs. Amoebic cysts have a tendency to linger.

Giardia
This year's designer diarrhoea caused by the parasite Giardia Lamblia.
Symptoms
Noisy rumbling stomach flatulence, eggy tasting burps and loose bowel movements. Fever unlikely. Bowel movements may be watery.
Treatment
Metronidazole (Flagyl) 400mg. 4 tabs 1 time daily for 2-3 days.
Do not mix Flagyl with alcohol. Side effects cause metallic taste in mouth and nausea.

HEAT RELATED PROBLEMS
In the collective experience of my colleagues and myself this is the one area where we have witnessed the most distress and problems - far more than cold or altitude put together. Why this should be is, I feel, easily explained. Those new to altitude and cold are aware of their ignorance and the potential dangers, whether through the epic tales of other adventures, or via the media, who can give the impression that those who come off a mountain with all their toes intact and still able to breathe with both lungs must have a guardian angel. So advice on altitude and the cold is not only listened to but actively sought out. Usually, however, advice on heat and the sun is often only partially absorbed because most of us have experienced it, to some degree, before, and

our minds float off to the memory files and recall lying on the beach in Scunthorpe. Nobody appreciates the sun like us Brits; very nice, but a sunny day in Trekland offers almost no comparison to a day on the beach, or even a day under the continental sun.

The chances are that on trek you'll be up higher and nearer the equator. The atmosphere there is thinner, and continues to become thinner as you climb, offering little protection from ultraviolet (UV) radiation, the main cause of the problem. It gets worse because not only are we more open to direct radiation, but also from atmospheric scattering, which allows UV to punch through cloud. This is compounded by reflection - 100% in the case of snow, but sand and rocks will also reflect to a very high degree. Add to this that many antibiotics, cosmetics and even medical creams increase our sensitivity towards UV. Now consider that you'll be working harder, physically, than you have ever done on any beach and you'll start to appreciate the nature of the sun in Trekland. It may be the same one that shines over Brighton but it shines with a very wicked smile on its face.

Don't fall into the old "I take a good tan" trap, because whether you take a tan or not is no indicator of how much fluid, salts or minerals you need, or have lost, or how you will react to the sun on trek. Even if you develop a tan reading a holiday brochure, pamper yourself on trek as if you were a new-born, fair haired baby and avoid becoming the subject of two pages in your trek leader's report. You've worked hard for this holiday, and don't worry because even smothered in factor 15 you'll still go home brown!

Protection
Protection is easy. Just cover up, either by clothing, which should be loose, or by using creams or blocks. Having talked about clothing, let's look at creams. Creams come in various grades, factor 1 being low protection, and at the moment, factor 32 being the maximum. Factor 15 seems to offer good general protection with factor 20 for those sensitive areas - noses and ears. For lips a total-block lip salve, if it's used liberally, keeps herpes away from those carrying the virus. These are minimum factors, and as we are all different, are only a general indication. Information is not hard to find considering our national obsession with the sun, and every local chemist can give you advice regarding your skin type, hair colour etc. If in doubt always be in favour of a higher factor.

Above the snow-line you really should be using a total block and covering all the areas normally in the shade - under the nose and chin and even behind the ears. Browning gently on a sun-bed prior to your trek is of little use as your skin will still be susceptible to a high-volume UV pounding

Sun hats and shades are covered under "Equipment", but let me reiterate the importance of well-fitting 100% UV block sun-glasses. Snow blindness can also be read as sand blindness. It is incredibly painful, has potentially long lasting effects, is easily contracted but is so easily avoided. Yes, good quality sun-glasses are expensive, but quality lasts, which is more than can be said for your eyes in the sun.

Hyperthermia due to sunburn
Cause

This occurs when you have been careless enough to let the sun and heat play directly on your skin. Skin should **always** be covered when you are out in the sun, either with appropriate clothing or a thick coating of high factor sun block or cream.

Effects

The sun will burn you as deep and as sure as a flame, and the effects are the same - blisters, red and marked skin, dehydration, nausea, sickness, headaches, diarrhoea and even shock. The body's thermostat can get a big shake up after sunstroke, with victims often going into fits of almost uncontrollable shivering as well as feeling extremely cold, especially after the sun has gone down. Body temperature can rise above 104°F (40°C) at which point consider the condition extreme and treat as described under "Extreme Hyperthermia".

Treatment

Rest, fluids, fluids and more fluids. Pain and headaches (usually caused by dehydration) can be treated with two or three aspirins. Blistered skin should be left alone. If blisters do burst then the wound should be covered with a sterile, greasy, antibiotic-impregnated gauze such as Bactigras or similar. I have seen antibiotic capsules broken open and dusted over a bad burn and the wound bound in food-wrap film. Crude, but effective, as any open wound is very prone to infection. Forget old wives' tales of spreading on butter etc, although if the skin is not broken "After sun" creams or even hand cream are very soothing, and are worth using for their physical and psychological relief, regardless of whether they have any medical benefit. Finally, a sachet or two of ORS will help replace those lost salts and minerals.

Prevention

Drink copiously. Pinch the skin as you are walking - if the pinched skin stays puckered and discoloured then cover up, slow down and drink. Cover up with either clothing (loose) or sun block. Don't jeopardise your health and everybody else's holiday by using low factor creams for the sake of a tan. High factors (15+) are the only way to go, especially near the equator and high up. This applies to everyone, not only those with fair skins. Remember to put cream on those not so obvious places - the back of the neck, the calves, ears, noses and the back of the hands. Horrible as it may seem, keep the skin feeling greasy. And drink!

Hyperthermia due to excess heat

Causes

The basic cause is over-heating due to indirect heat. Usually because the cooling radiator is allowed to run dry, ie. low fluid intake. Over-dressing is another reason, and is easily resolved. Not so obvious is the hair-dryer effect of warm breezes; whilst pleasant on the skin, they dehydrate the body (causing over-heating) very quickly and surreptitiously.

Effects

As a close cousin to sunstroke, heatstroke shares many of its characteristics - high temperature, nausea, headaches, sometimes diarrhoea and in extreme cases fluid retention in the limbs and / or shock. Shivers and feeling cold may follow.

Treatment

You know what I'm going to say, don't you? Fluids, fluids and more fluids. Take aspirin for headaches, mild anti-acid for nausea, and rest. Fluid retention is nature's way of trying to combat heatstroke and unless it is extremely uncomfortable (often fluid gathers round the feet and ankles) it should be left to dissipate naturally. Put your feet up when resting in the evening. However, if it has reached the point of disabling the individual, or the skin is stretched to the point of pain rather than discomfort, it can be drained by means of drugs but only if the other symptoms have passed. The reason for this is that the only drugs that will have the desired effect are strong diuretics such as Lasix which will drain the body indiscriminately, undoing all the good of the fluids you poured in earlier to counteract the initial symptoms. So it's ironic that after you've administered the diuretic you must back it up with copious amounts of fluid. And, of course, ORS. They are very quick-acting, however, and relief is fairly rapid, even if it feels as if your bladder has assumed proportions akin to the Aswan Dam. Rest and elevate legs. Lasix (Frusemide), if necessary, should be administered as follows: 1 x 40mg tablet and repeat once six hours later. If no improvement (unlikely) then repeat the following day. After two days retreat and find medical advice. If there are any other symptoms, such as headache, confusion or breathlessness, descend and seek medical advice as quickly as possible.

Prevention

Don't be lazy: take off and put on layers of clothes as the day goes on, so that you maintain as comfortable a temperature as possible. If need be rest in the shade. Don't try to walk at a pace that's uncomfortably fast for you. Keep your head covered with a loose broad-brimmed hat and if possible soak it now and again (luxury!) And drink.

Extreme Hyperthermia
Causes

As before but with a temperature at or above 104°F (40°C). Unconsciousness may follow and if so the patient's condition must be treated as an emergency.
Effects

Over-heating your body for any amount of time will increase the risk of permanent damage to your kidneys and liver, brain, heart and intestines. Two hours' unconsciousness makes permanent damage a probability, if you survive.
Treatment

Nature must be helped to cool the body as it obviously isn't managing by itself, so any obvious methods should be used - place in the shade, remove clothing, create (or find) a cool breeze, apply wet (cool, not cold) cloths, immerse in cool (not cold!) water. Stop when the patient's temperature drops to 102°F and only continue if it proceeds to rise again. Over-enthusiasm in cooling the patient below 102°F may result in you having to read the section on hypothermia!! Prevention - as before.

Muscle cramp
Cause

Lack of salt - isotonic discrepancy.
Effects

Extremely painful and stiff muscles, particularly the calves and thighs.
Treatment

Massaging the affected area is often all that's needed. With big muscles like the thighs this may have to be quite vigorous but avoid pummelling or you may have to treat for other pain!

Drink profusely, but make sure you've added ORS or any other isotonic supplement.
Prevention

Avoid dehydration and working cold muscles - remember your warm-up exercises. And drink!

Chafing/sweat rashes
Cause

Friction, usually where one skin surface moves over another, or where two skin surfaces touch. The skin in question can either be very dry, or rather clammy, ie. sweaty.

Effects

Localised areas of sore, tender skin which can lead to a rash and even infection. Favourite hotspots are: the armpits, inner thighs, behind the knees and around the anus.

Treatment

If the skin is unbroken then a liberal layer of petroleum jelly will keep things sliding smoothly. If broken then treat as a graze - apply antiseptic cream and cover with a clean dressing.

Prevention

Maintain as high a standard of personal hygiene as conditions will allow and powder potential areas at night. Apply powder or petroleum jelly in the morning. As with blisters, take action as soon as the first symptoms appear.

Blisters

This is a friction burn usually avoided by wearing a proven sock/boot combination. Blisters can occur if your feet become wet, swollen or even shrink! Hotspots will give a first warning and it's possible to pre-empt the blister by covering with broad zinc-oxide tape.

If you miss this opportunity and a blister forms try to leave it overnight before covering. Obviously if camp is still six hours away then immediate action must be taken. One should try to avoid bursting the blister but in 90% of cases this is impractical, so do so carefully by washing then piercing it twice, with a sterile needle, at the bottom, and aid fluid evacuation by gently rolling the needle across the blister, down towards the holes. Try not to tear the blister and expose the flesh underneath, as this will increase the risk of infection, as will contact with your fingers. Should this happen, then dust with antibiotic powder or smear with antiseptic cream. Cut a "Melolin" or similar patch to the shape of the blister, but 3mm larger all round, smear with antiseptic cream, and fix over the blister with zinc-oxide tape. This should overlap and extend 2-3cm beyond the patch. Prior to replacing the sock, warm the tape with your hands, which makes the glue on the tape soft, and rub gently so that the tape adopts the contours of the affected area and is well adhered at the edges. The skin must be dry to allow this. Replace the sock and boot and tighten sufficiently, so as not to allow the boot to move and rub, but slack enough to prevent the patient from fainting with pain.

If conditions allow, soak the tape and remove it each evening, and allow air around the blister during the night, replacing the dressing in the morning. If you are in tough country, in less than ideal circumstances, then providing there is no sign of infection - swelling with a hot sensation - leave the dressing as it is until such times as you can get access to it.

There are a couple of excellent products - "2nd skin" and "moleskin" plaster - which will do just as good a job, but I prefer the zinc-oxide method because it uses readily available, inexpensive materials common to most first-aid kits.

Skin cancer
Caused by prolonged exposure (years) to sunlight. Skin cancer is easy to detect early on in its process. It's worth a mention because so many people don't consider it a British problem. But with the way our atmosphere is thinning it is likely to become more predominant. Also, you just don't know how much time you are going to spend in the sun. Which straw did break the camel's back? Besides, prevention is so easy, just cover up - lotion or clothes, the choice is yours.

COLD RELATED PROBLEMS
Most cold related problems are caused by scant thought rather than scant clothing. Being aware of the problems and how to avoid them helps you to stay adequately and safely warm. Think of the body as a stove and our clothing as insulation. First, there is no heat without fire and the fuel required here is food, and lots of it. But of the right kind - lots of sugars and easily absorbed high-energy fuels like honey and chocolate, dried fruit and glucose sweets. Proteins are not as easily digested as carbohydrates, so plenty of pasta but easy on the steaks. Clothes have been mentioned, so just a quick recap on how to use them.

Dressing in layers allows fine temperature control - but only if you make the effort to carry enough clothing and to put them on as you begin to cool (lagging the stove). At the beginning of the day this is not usually a problem; early mornings without the sun tend to compel you to dress up. As the day goes on, clothes come off and the rucksack gets bigger. Most people start to chill down as early evening approaches. When you're feeling tired, with lunch three hours ago, camp one hour away, and a damp sweat on the body and in the clothes, replacing clothing seems to become a chore. But this is a dangerous time because the body will cool down as quick as the shadows draw across the valleys, especially as cold air is drawn down off the tops, and the fire is only ticking over on its embers. Cold weakens the body; it uses valuable energy in an effort to keep warm. This is energy that can be best used in other ways.

The moisture we create as we work is a significant factor in our keeping warm. Its function is to cool us down, but lingering sweat will create damp clothing which will continue to cool long after we want it to, especially in a cold wind or breeze. Cotton clothing is especially prone to this, as it clings to the skin when damp, rendering it useless, so a layer of non-absorbant fabric close to the skin which will wick away sweat is essential.

With thought and a careful selection of layers, it is possible to maintain dry clothes. Our feet, however, are harder to keep dry. Plastic boots and efficient gaiters will ward off water from the outside, but are very little help in preventing perspiration. Damp feet create all sorts of problems from "Athlete's Foot" to "Trench Foot" but damp feet in extreme cold creates frostbite, often becoming gangrenous. Dry socks and boots are the solution and a supply of clean dry socks must be available to give feet a chance. This requires vigilance and self-discipline to maintain. Always carry a dry pair of socks in your rucksack. Your toes will be grateful, as will the rest of your body, especially at night.

Hypothermia due to exposure
Causes

Nature has evolved a very special way of protecting a human's vital organs - heart, lungs, liver, kidneys and brain - as things start to cool off: it shuts down the heat supply to the less vital parts, the peripheries, in an effort to maintain body temperature in our core. The short-term effects of this are slight, little more than discomfort. But if these measures to preserve warmth are not enough then the core itself starts to cool and things become serious. As a body struggles to create or preserve its own heat, the heart will start to slow down and the body temperature will drop, until eventually the heart will cease to work at all. As the heart starts to slow down, blood supply to the vitals will too, including the brain, producing huge swings in mood and temperament, ataxia and poor psycho-motor coordination.

Effects

As an indication to the severity of a hypothermic person's condition, the following is a rough guide:

Mild Hypothermia 98°F-90°F (37°C-32°C)
1. Shivering, cold feelings, some coordination problems.
2. Above symptoms more obvious, stumbling and general listlessness.
3. Balance and physical coordination severely affected, loss of manual dexterity and slow mental processes.

Severe Hypothermia 90°F-82°F (32°C-28°C)
1. Shivering stops, little muscle coordination, confusion and irritable behaviour.
2. Semi-conscious, dilated pupils, immobile.
3. Unconscious, leading to death.

It would be a mistake to presume that the rate at which hypothermia strikes is proportional to air temperature. The equation is greatly affected by two other factors: the wind and the ambient moisture content. It's the "Chill Factor", a phenomenon that means if it's cold, windy and damp then you'll chill down a lot, lot quicker than if it's just cold and damp, or windy and damp. People have produced impressive charts stating exactly (almost) how quickly you chill down, under which circumstances. Unless you have a photographic memory they'll do no more good than impress on you that you lose a lot of heat when it's cold, blowing and damp.

An individual suffering from hypothermia will experience a deterioration in both physical and mental performance, the latter preventing them from either recognising their condition or being able to redress the balance. The onus is therefore on the other members of the group to monitor each other, and act on any individual's behalf to arrest their condition and restore them to full working order should the signs and symptoms be present.

Most of us cool down when we stop to rest or finish for the day, but being chilly whilst walking is a bad, bad sign, especially for more than ten minutes or so. As the body continues to chill down, muscular performance dulls, manifesting itself in sluggish movements, stumbling and general lethargy. Allowed to continue, the lethargy will progress to become a complete disregard for one's own condition, or a refusal to accept anything is wrong at all. Falling, uncontrollable shivering, poor hand-to-eye coordination and slow or slurred speech may occur. The next steps, confusion and amnesia, follow, marking the border between Mild and Severe Hypothermia.

Before losing consciousness a hypothermic person's mental abilities become extremely impaired and they should never be left unattended as it is not uncommon for casualties to remove clothing whilst in this state. Unfortunately, persuading them to stay warm can present problems as individuals can also become very uncooperative. By this stage a hypothermic candidate is unlikely, physically, to be able to walk or even stand unaided, and will be drifting rapidly towards unconsciousness.

Mild Hypothermia - treatment
Stop the heat loss. This is easy: find or create shelter, throw on lots of dry clothes and wind and waterproofs, woolly hat and fleecy gloves. Next, create heat by stoking up the boiler with food and sweet drinks, and if the cool body in question is not too bad, keep exercising, especially the legs as they contain our biggest muscles and create most heat. Once the temperature is up, and the symptoms have apparently gone, be vigilant to ensure there is no regression - remember to keep stoking the fire, as a brief time spent in a hypothermic state will severely reduce a body's reserves.

Severe Hypothermia - treatment

Stop the heat loss as before and think seriously about evacuation. Trying to reheat the core when the body has all but lost its own ability to do so is a very hit and miss affair, even in this age of medical enlightenment. Just to compound these problems the heart has a tendency to fibrillate when cold which can also be triggered by jerky or rough movements, such as those that occur in stretcher evacuations. As Dr James A. Wilkerson says, "Hypothermia is to be avoided, not treated".

The biggest problem about reheating when the core has dropped below 90°F (32°C) is that it must be heated from the inside out. By warming the peripheries (for example rubbing the hands, or placing feet on a hot water bottle) a process of basic physics draws warm(ish) blood from the core to replace it with the even colder blood from the extremities, further cooling and increasing the risk of fibrillation. Of course the extremities must remain insulated to prevent further heat loss, but reheating must come from within. A warm, moist airstream must be inhaled to heat the blood vessels of the lungs, so put up the tent, put the kettle on and crowd everyone round the casualty, because that person has now become a casualty. Chemical warm packs can be applied to the side of the rib cage and neck. (Although we have intimate knowledge of the physiological effects of hypothermia we are very much in the dark as to how to treat it. Don't give up when all seems lost. If nothing else we, as a race, are remarkably resilient and recoveries have been made by individuals against all medical expectation.)

Prevention

If you've laboured through the previous paragraphs then methods of prevention should be apparent. I have been lucky enough to have witnessed only two cases of hypothermia, both mild, and both instances the result of a fall into cold water. The first was after a canoe capsized, but the second was after a river crossing, when despite having been in the river for only a minute and a half maximum, and only immersed to the waist, my friend chilled down to the point of showing those first scary signs: shivering listlessness and non-cooperation. What prevented his condition from deteriorating was our party's vigilance. His recovery was swift.

Frostbite

Cause

Frostbite occurs when the skin tissue freezes. The areas most susceptible are those with the poorest circulation: the peripheries and those most often exposed - the ears, nose, lips and cheeks. The process of frostbite will be accelerated if the core is struggling to maintain its temperature, as described in the previous pages, leaving poor circulation to the peripheries. Left unchecked the area of frozen tissue will expand and will freeze deeper, making recovery harder, and increasing the risk of permanent damage.

Effect

Initially frostbite is very painful, the pain being one of its first symptoms, but as the skin tissues freeze, all sensation is lost. The skin appears white and is, naturally, very cold to touch. As it develops the frozen area will enlarge and become hard to touch - just like a lump of frozen meat, which it has, in fact, become. The frozen tissue may take on a purple hue as the frostbite deepens. Mild frostbite or "frost nip" is usually restricted to small localised areas - the tip of the nose or a toe or finger tip, and if recognised and covered quickly will thaw quickly too and recover well, leaving an area of red as opposed to white skin. Illustrations of frostbite usually picture what look like ten blackened chipolata sausages, with only bits of nail to give a clue as to their origin, and this is what will come out of your boots if frostbite is left unchecked for a week or so. The black covering of dead tissue is called "eschar" and is not a good sign....

I've witnesses idiots with frostbite waggling their frozen digits around as if they were some kind of mark of achievement in mountaineering. For a description of the true nature of the condition and its effects, read Herzog's *Annapurna* - you'll never go anywhere without gloves again. (The book should be read anyway as it is a mountaineering classic.)

Treatment

For effective recovery the frozen area must be defrosted fully and quickly, but only if there is a guarantee that the affected area will not be refrozen. Freezing, thaw, and refreezing will only further the extent of the damage. This is best done by immersion into warm (100°F-108°F [38°C-42°C]) water. As the frozen appendage warms, the water will cool and a supply of hot water must be available to maintain the heat. Temperature must, of course, be monitored by someone other than the casualty, bearing in mind their loss of feeling. A rough guide to the water temperature is that an uninjured hand can be immersed in the water comfortably. It is common sense that the affected area will be removed from the water, whilst it is being topped up, and that it should never be heated directly - the idea being to thaw out the casualty, not cook them! Slow reheating, for example by exposing to the sun, is not advisable as it can lead to the complication of infection and uneven thawing. Reheating must be quick to be effective and to offer a hope of rapid recovery and minimal permanent damage.

Reheating should take between 30 minutes and an hour, when the tissue should become soft and pliable. If not, keep going until it is. Blisters may form giving an indication as to the damage done - if they contain clear fluid things are looking good: a bloody fluid implies permanent tissue damage. No blistering and a retained purple hue signifies severe damage. The reheating process is very painful and providing the sufferer has no other injuries that would react adversely, painkillers can be administered to ease the situation.

Once reheating has taken place, the damaged tissues must be protected to prevent further damage from either refreezing or rubbing against clothing or bedding. Evacuation to hospital is the only sensible option as recovery can take weeks, if not months. The affected areas must be kept clean by soaking daily in disinfected warm water, and covered with a sterile dressing. Should the damaged skin become infected then antibiotics (Ampicillin or Ciproxin) can be admnistered, but apart from the comfort afforded by painkillers there are no drugs that can be administered in the field to accelerate the healing process.

Prevention

The circulation to the peripheries must be maintained by ensuring that the core is adequately provided for and that clothing, especially on the hands and feet, provide adequate insulation, whilst not being so tight as to cut off circulation. Feet in particular are prone to this kind of restricted circulation due to overtightening of the laces and too many pairs of socks being worn. Remember that if you want to push more heat out to the hands and feet, put on another jumper and a woolly hat! Surplus heat from the core will go out to the peripheries. Modern plastic boots with their hyper-efficient, space-age inner boots and non-moisture absorbing outers have reduced the odds of frostbite greatly for the modern mountaineer, but remember those dry socks. Trapped sweat in the boot will freeze.

Protect the face with a thick Balaclava or ski mask, or if you know that you are going to be in an extremely cold environment for any duration, a purpose-made neoprene face mask. Be vigilant and look out for yourself and others. Whilst a frost-nipped finger can be quickly thawed out under the arm pit, ignored, it can rapidly become frost-bitten to the point where it will literally fall off.

Snow blindness

Snow blindness is caused by reflected UV light burning the cornea. The symptoms are not always felt immediately, often eight to twelve hours later, but when they are, they are extremely painful. Moving or blinking the eye, or even exposure to light can cause severe pain. The eyelids may also become red and swollen. Initial irritation in the eye will give way to the feeling of hot grit under the lids. Treat with an eye patch which stops the friction rub of the eyelid opening and closing and allows the delicate skin of the cornea to heal in about forty-eight hours. In addition, cold compresses, dark glasses or a dark environment, and antibiotic eye ointment applied four times daily may be beneficial.

Until recently the standard practice was to anaesthetise the eyes using Amethocaine (0.5ml). This is frowned upon now because there is danger of damaging the eye when it is anaesthetised and the Amethocaine itself may slow up the healing process. Prevention is by means of close fitting, 100% UV filtered glacier spectacles or goggles.

ALTITUDE RELATED ILLNESSES
About altitude
If the following information reads to you like a catalogue of horrors and does nothing but deter you from trekking up high then I am truly sorry, and I have failed in one of my objectives - to arm you, as a trekker, with the confidence to travel to altitude and experience the outdoors in this unique environment.

The sun rising and setting at altitude is without parallel; the colours are from the very edge of God's palette and the air has a clarity that feels as though it might shatter. Only up high can you feel the curve of the earth and view a thousand peaks twixt you and the horizon. Acclimatised, you become aware of your body, of your being, in a way you've never done before, or will again...until you climb up there once more.

This information is strength. It could help you save another's life - don't let it deject or deter you. Remember, all these conditions are avoidable by taking four things: time, water, aspirin, and more time.

Our bodies trap oxygen in our lungs and transfer it to our blood. From here it whizzes round our body doing all the good things blood does. The process of transferring the oxygen from lung to blood is dependent on the concentration of the oxygen in the lungs being greater than that of the blood cells. At 5,500m (18,000ft) the atmospheric pressure is half of what it is at sea level but the blood's need for oxygen is the same. So, to try and maintain the oxygen level we breathe harder, although no matter how hard you breathe it is never the same as at sea level. Decreased oxygen pressure resulting in less blood-borne oxygen is compensated for by the heart increasing circulation, raising the heart-rate. It is this oxygen deficiency that accounts for most of the problems that occur when going up high.

The fact that climbers can, and do, stand on the highest summits of the world without supplementary oxygen proves that our bodies will adapt to working with less available oxygen. This is acclimatisation, and provided that sufficient time is given to allow the body to make its necessary adaptation, then it is possible to side-step most of the dangers and much of the discomfort of gaining height.

Individuals acclimatise at different rates - this is a physiological problem. Our bodies mostly work in the same way, but each of us has our own idiosyncrasies. The rules of acclimatisation are therefore general but the principles apply to all, and if the figures don't suit you, or if you haven't suffered any of the side-effects of going up high, then don't think for a moment that you are immune, because no one is.

Few walkers or mountaineers suffer below 2,500m and most manage to 3,000m without problems. If there are no problems at 3,000m ascend to 3,500m the next day and then to 4,000m the following day. From 4,000m onwards reduce the daily rate of ascent to 300m per day, reduced to 150m if you feel discomfort. Every third or fourth day should be a rest day. There is an adage amongst mountaineers, "climb high and sleep low", and this is good advice borne out of experience. It is perfectly acceptable, for example, to start the day at 4,000m, climb to 5,000m and finish the day at 4,300m. This is an excellent way to attain acclimatisation, and stay within the rules.

The effects of altitude usually manifest themselves twelve to twenty-four hours after attaining altitude at 3,000-3,500m. This is no reason to panic; if you ascend as by the "rules", then the effects should start to wear off after three days, the symptoms being worse on day one or two. If they don't, then think again about climbing any higher, consider dropping 600m, have a good night's sleep, then start again. Often anxiety, dehydration and ignorance can create symptoms similar to Acute Mountain Sickness (AMS). So relax, and enjoy the view from way-up-there.

There is no chemical substitute for acclimatisation, although Diamox (Acetazolamide) is used by some as an aid to relieve a few of the symptoms and is claimed by some to actually prevent AMS. The biggest danger is that because Diamox makes you feel good, you will ignore the basic rules, go too high, too quick and bring on AMS, or worse. In the past it was thought necessary to initiate using Diamox prior to going up to altitude. This is now deemed to be unnecessary. It is recommended that it is only used as the symptoms of altitude manifest themselves. Diamox can have some very uncomfortable side-effects - increased urine output (necessitating an increased fluid intake), tingling sensation in the fingers, toes, or cheeks and possibly restricted vision. It is worth taking some at home as a test to see if you are prone to any, or all of the aforementioned. The recommended dosage is 250mg (one tablet) every twelve hours, for three days.

A drug that has been used prophylactically for many years to seemingly good effect is aspirin - but only aspirin, as only it thins the blood. A 300mg tablet taken at night seems to relieve the headaches and reduces the risk of venous thrombosis (blood clots) in the extremities and pulmonary emboli - blood clots in the lung. Aspirin should be administered to all suffering any altitude related conditions for these reasons. The small dose over a short time seems worth the risk unless there are contra-indications: children under twelve years or a trekker with stomach ulceration, asthma or aspirin allergy. In many countries locals chew garlic as an aid to acclimatisation. Fine, as long as your tent-mate does too! I have a friend who takes garlic capsules nightly up high and swears that they help him to acclimatise...and why shouldn't it?

The dangerous things to take up high are sleeping tablets and strong painkillers, which can mask symptoms and suppress the respiratory system, already slower at night, hindering acclimatisation and creating the false impression that all is well. Alcohol and smoking, as stimulants, increase the strain on the already stressed heart, and in the case of smoking restrict the dilation of the arteries, reducing blood flow. Committed smokers will argue that because a smoker is used to less oxygen in the system their bodies adapt very quickly to the rarefied atmosphere. Maybe so, but they also have heart attacks and die, which could be an encumbrance on the rest of the group. Bottled oxygen is very helpful to have up high, but for the volume needed is very bulky and expensive. It must be administered for at least 15 minutes to have any effect at all, and a low dose over a long period is far more beneficial than a quick burst at a high dose. I witnessed a Sherpa going round the tents of one trekking group just before everyone retired offering them a quick whiff before going to sleep. Everyone took it, and swore blind to me it helped. They were camped at 3,500m.... A "D" size bottle of oxygen which contains 340 litres is about the minimum size of bottle to carry if being used for emergencies - this gives two to three hours' supply and weighs about 15lbs. A close fitting mask must accompany it. It is also very expensive. A "D" refill costs about £76 in the UK.

Not many trekking groups carry oxygen but many now carry "Gammov Bags" - a portable pressure chamber that can simulate 600m of descent and folds to the size of a daysack. They can be hired in Kathmandu for very moderate fees, but even the purchase price - some $2,000 - is a paltry sum for an expedition and nothing compared to the price of a life.

Acute Mountain Sickness (AMS) - Mild

AMS is the collective term given to a whole group of unpleasant symptoms associated with high altitude. The danger is not from their appearance but from ignoring them, especially if they become more persistent. These symptoms may include nausea and sickness, loss of appetite, mild shortness of breath with exertion, light or broken sleep, irregular breathing especially at night, dizziness, lassitude, swelling of face and hands, and headaches. All of these are avoidable by acclimatising properly and are due to the lack of oxygen. It is not uncommon for trekkers to suffer from one or two of these symptoms for a few hours or even a day or two. The official line from the medical world is that unless you can conclusively prove that symptoms shown are not AMS related then they must be viewed as such and the trekker must descend until they disappear before ascending again. End of story. Or so it should be. In the real world, people are very reluctant to descend, especially those on a once-in-a-lifetime adventure or those who don't like to complain or feel that they would hold back the group, so symptoms are disguised - easy to do if you don't spend all day beside a person - until the condition deteriorates to the point of being undisguisable and impossible to conceal making evacuation a necessity.

Some trek leaders come to an uncomfortable compromise. As their groups begin to enter into high altitude, about 4,000m, a deal is struck. If members of the group promise to be honest about their symptoms and they are showing only two or three, then they won't be sent down straight away, but will be given until lunch-time that day to ascertain whether their symptoms are easing off or getting worse. Should they feel the same, or worse, then down they go. Most of us descend about two to four times quicker than we ascend, so it is possible, in half a day, to be well below that morning's starting point. Descending over 300m can have an amazing and dramatic effect on a mild AMS sufferer's condition. Recovery is often rapid (one day) and once the symptoms have cleared it is safe to ascend again with caution. Should the symptoms ease considerably to become little more than a nuisance then, for that day at least, they are allowed to continue. It is a deal I've struck in the past, and whilst the responsibility of allowing a case of mild AMS to go on against medical advice is frightening, knowing that the group is being honest is a comfort. If you think this is an irresponsible attitude, try seeing what happens when you lay down the law - people clam up, and observant as the best may be, they may not always spot the one with AMS early on, when it can be easily counteracted. Two suggestions have been offered to me as to why this deal actually does work. One is that because people feel there is a little lee-way then they become more relaxed and avoid anxiety-borne symptoms such as nausea and headaches. The other is that at night our metabolism slows down at altitude. This means that the acclimatisation process slows down too. This starts to reactivate when you wake and begin to move about a bit, and speeds up a gear when the exercise starts. So for many, first thing in the morning is not a fair time to make absolute judgement, as those first few hours of the day can see a huge improvement in a person's physiological condition. For some of us the rules apply at sea-level.... The final word must be that if there is any doubt at any time, then the decision is to go down! I am not advocating flaunting the rules at all; it's a bit like doctors giving drug addicts clean needles in an effort to make a dangerous habit a little less dangerous without in any way encouraging or condoning drug taking.

Those who ignore the warning of mild AMS, or climb too high much too quickly, are candidates for severe AMS, and when you reach this level there are no compromises or deals. It's a case of getting down as fast as possible, and keeping those fingers crossed.

Acute Mountain Sickness - Severe

The symptoms for severe AMS are: constant painful headaches, regular bouts of vomiting, lack of understanding, drowsiness, ataxia (poor physical coordination), coughing - with or without producing phlegm or blood, severe lethargy, cyanosis (blueness around face and lips) and difficulty breathing (after mild exertion or at rest) and a very high resting pulse - 120 beats per minute or higher.

Severe AMS, like hypothermia, warrants the others in the group making decisions on the sufferer's behalf. As AMS affects the brain, the sufferer's judgement or understanding of the situation must, to be on the safe side, be presumed to be unreliable, and the sufferer is no longer able to be held accountable for his/her own health or safety.

Ataxia is considered to be the cross-over point between mild and severe AMS. It is easily tested by asking the sufferer to walk heel to toe along a straight line for 15ft; or stand, arms by the side with the eyes shut and feet together without swaying considerably, or having to move the feet apart to maintain balance. Compare this to the performance of a non-sufferer. Ataxic trekkers should start descending immediately, preferably under their own steam, and regardless of the time of day. THEY MUST BE ACCOMPANIED. If relief isn't quick enough (within twenty-four hours maximum) unconsciousness will follow, death shortly after that. Keep descending until recovery or until you hit the beach...recovery will have involved a close shave and medical help and rest are priorities. After a bout of AMS going back up to altitude immediately is not recommended.

Prevention

Proper and complete acclimatisation. Ascending at the correct and comfortable rate. Aspirin and Diamox should be administered. Losing height quickly has a very high success rate.

High Altitude Cerebral Edema (HACE)

Edema is a build-up of fluid and in the case of HACE, around the brain. The reasons why it occurs are complex and a little open to conjecture but are definitely traceable to hypoxia (lack of oxygen) and/or vasoconstriction. HACE can cause temporary (or permanent) brain damage and death.

Ataxia is the principal symptom of HACE, alongside severe persistent headaches, poor mental functions and possible nausea. The headache may require painkillers (aspirin) and the mental impairment can range from confusion to amnesia through to psychotic behaviour. As in AMS, the Ataxia seems to primarily affect balance, but secondary symptoms will affect simple hand/eye movements such as drinking, using zips or tying laces.

HACE is not an extension of AMS although it can follow on from it, but can be contracted quite independently of any other condition.

As in all altitude related illnesses descent is the best treatment and with HACE it is a priority. Dexamethazone can be administered - 4mg four times a day. If used longer than a period of five days then the dose must be gradually reduced under medical supervision to avoid steroid psychosis. If oxygen is available then administer it at 2 litres per minute. Other than that little else can be done. Evenings and mornings seem to be the worst time for HACE and therefore the best time to check each other for symptoms.

Prevention through acclimatisation and careful monitoring of each other is really much better than trying to find a cure - being up high really is a time to be careful, but HACE rarely hits well acclimatised trekkers.

High Altitude Pulmonary Edema (HAPE)

Here edema fluid collects in the lungs. The result is an inability to assimilate sufficient oxygen in the bloodstream. The less efficient the process becomes, the more oxygen it requires to function, a downward efficiency curve which falls out very steeply. Once a sufferer becomes comatose, death is likely to follow within six to twelve hours, despite being a pulmonary condition, because of oxygen starvation to the brain. There are many psychotic symptoms which are similar to that of HACE. However, careful observation must be carried out as HAPE can progress very quickly, particularly as the metabolism slows down at night. Caught in time and treated with nothing other than descent, recovery from HAPE is likely and full. It has been categorised into four classes.

1. Mild - pulse less than 110 per minute with respiratory rate of less than 20 per minute. The main symptoms are difficulty gaining breath after exertion. Rales (crackling sound heard from lungs - usually heard with a stethoscope) may be present.
2. Moderate - pulse 110-120 per minute with respiratory rate of 20-30. Symptoms: breathless, dry cough, rales, headache, rales often heard with naked ear, and extreme tiredness after little effort.
3. Serious - pulse 120-130 per minute with respiratory rate of 30. Symptoms: breathless, weak, extreme persistent headache, persistent cough possibly producing phlegm, lack of appetite, rales.
4. Severe - pulse greater than 130 per minute with respiratory rate 40.

Symptoms: stupor or coma, psychosis, purple on lips, face and nails, rales phlegm or sputum, possibly containing blood.

Treatment

The first course of action for all classes of pulmonary edema is rapid descent - as much and as quickly as possible, and at least 1,000m. If oxygen is carried then administer it at 2 litres per minute after an initial bust of 15 minutes at 4 to 6 litres. Administer oxygen for six hours if possible and twelve if supplies permit. If a helicopter evacuation has been arranged then ensure that it carries oxygen - remember, the helicopter has to gain altitude before it can descend. The patient will feel most comfortable sitting up.

Administer aspirin (salicylic acid) - two tablets (600mg) twice a day. This thins the blood and reduces the risk of pulmonary emboli (blood clots on the lung). Check beforehand that the patient is not allergic to aspirin, or is asthmatic, since aspirin can affect the condition.

If the pulmonary edema has been diagnosed by a physician to have been caused by a heart related illness then administer Lasix (Frusemide): 40-80mg initially, as directed by the doctor.

For HAPE, Nifedipine is about the only drug around that seems to have any marked effect - initially 10mg. If there is no progress administer another 10mg two hours later, then another 5-20mg per day, depending on the severity of the condition, until the condition stabilises. For immediate effect bite the capsule and let the liquid stay under the tongue. Nifedipine is no substitute for descent and should only be used in conjunction with it. A litter evacuation is necessary in every case other than one of mild symptoms.

Other ailments attributed to altitude

Systemic Edema

Many people experience a slight swelling of the face, hands and feet, and occasionally the abdomen at altitude - this should be of little concern unless the symptoms become severe. Ascending shouldn't be a problem but remove rings and tight bangles just to be on the safe side.

Immune Suppression

Cuts, grazes and infection seem to take forever to heal at altitude - but just keep them clean and apply antiseptic cream until you get down low and they will heal up. If they do become a problem then descend.

Sleep Problems

Little or poor sleep at altitude is common, and unless you are getting absolutely no sleep at all, has to be grinned and borne. Sleeping tablets at altitude are out because most suppress the respiratory system. If exhaustion from lack of sleep is imminent then descend for a rest.

A common phenomenon at altitude is Cheyne-Stokes (periodic) breathing. When this occurs, the sufferer's breathing rate becomes progressively slower until it almost stops...it then returns quickly back to normal, only to become progressively slower...repeat cycle. Usually the sufferer is asleep and blissfully unaware of what's happening. It's hell for the poor person sharing their tent. An indescribable variation is Cheyne-Stokes snoring which keeps a whole camp awake and on tenterhooks. Bruises to the face and abdomen are common - inflicted by completely frazzled tent-mates! Other than this, it is generally harmless. I call it "Father's Fall-out", after sharing a tent with my dad....

High Altitude Flatulence (HAF)
This is a common, but noisy condition and harmless provided no-one smokes inside the tent. There is nothing that can be done to prevent it and relief is natural. And you thought those noises outside were bullfrogs....

High Altitude Cough (Khumbu Cough)
This irritating dry cough is caused by dry, dusty or cold air irritating the tissues of the back of the throat, and of the bronchi. Unless accompanied by a fever it is unlikely to be an infection and it's therefore unnecessary to take antibiotics. Better relief is gained from sucking throat lozenges.

Children at altitude
Young people are more prone to AMS and other altitude related conditions, principally due to their acclimatising slower than adults, and often their lack of experience, or inability to communicate, masks any abnormal signs or symptoms. Allow under 12s at least twice as long to acclimatise, and ensure that each child has a dedicated medical/drug list - adult doses can (**do**) and will kill a child with perhaps a body weight one-tenth that of an adult. Never give aspirin to any child under twelve years old. This is not to say that children should not be taken up high, but the adult has to accept that the decision for them to go up high is the adult's, not the child's - informed choice from little ones doesn't really come into this equation. Just take your time.

MARK'S STORY
I've included the following story to illustrate not only what can happen at

Health: Be prepared to improvise in the case of an accident.
A casualty being carried in the Rowaling Valley, Nepal

Well equipped porters reaching the Gondoro La, Pakistan. Layla Peak
and Gondogoro Glacier behind *(Author)*

An October storm in the Khumbu, Nepal. High altitude treks demand
good protective clothing *(W. Unsworth)*

altitude but also to demonstrate what an important role common sense plays up high. It first appeared in *High* magazine. I've also included part of a reply Mark received to his story the following month.

"We slumped in the snow drinking cocoa tea in an attempt to keep dehydration, and therefore headaches, at bay. We were at about 5,000m now, and supposedly on our way to climb the south-west face of Alpamayo. Dave said nothing although I suspected that I knew what he was thinking: he was not going to go any higher on this climbing trip. "I'm going down" he announced. Knowing Dave this was obviously not a snap decision but one he had thought through very carefully. I did not argue with him and try to persuade him to continue. He looked white and his lips were tinged with blue. There was no choice but to descend.

This was our third week in the Cordillera Blanca and despite careful and gradual acclimatisation Dave had felt consistently ill at 5,000m and above. He had resisted taking medication apart from an odd aspirin, wisely believing that if his body did not want to acclimatise then he should not bully it into submission by pumping it full of drugs.

So we descended the glacier and engaged in the inevitable procession of slides and tumbles down the moraine. Nearing the bottom we met three Frenchmen who appeared full of confidence - rather a contrast to our own states of mind. We explained the reason for our long faces. Immediately they claimed to have the solution "We 'ave Diamox, Monsieur". They explained that this had helped them to acclimatise on three previous expeditions. And besides, they were doctors. The invitation was to take Diamox and then climb Alpamayo. They appeared bemused by Dave's refusal to accept their offer. So off they went, talkative and continuing to be very happy.

Dave and I returned to Huaraz. He was dejected and decided to fly home as soon as he could obtain a flight. I chose to stay on to see if my luck would change. It did! I teamed up with a Swiss girl and returned to Alpamayo the next day. Having left my Alpamayo Base Camp only the previous day, I was back. (How this was achieved is another story.)

From the Base Camp we planned to move up to the Col, where we would bivy and try the route the following day. We arrived at the place where Dave and I had arrived at the decision to descend. I felt very sad and did not want to stay long at this spot. I looked up to the Col. I could just make out a group of people moving downwards, very slowly. Even with my none too wonderful eyesight it soon became apparent that there was a problem. It was another hour before we met the group. It consisted of six Spaniards congregated around a trussed up figure in a bivy bag whom they were dragging down the mountain. The barely conscious swollen faced figure was one of the French doctors. (Where his two friends were was a mystery.)

My new climbing partner, it just so happened, was a final year medical student doing her thesis on mountain sickness. Susi examined the Frenchman and could only urge the Spaniards to get him down the mountain immediately post-haste. This indeed must have been a frightening experience for him as he was tobogganed off down the ice, closely followed by six excited Spaniards.

To my mind Dave had been right. Diamox is not a substitute for acclimatization and short-cuts are dangerous in more ways than one.

Mark Seaton

Dear Mr Seaton

...people feel better and perform better on the drug (Diamox), oxygen levels are higher and muscle strength is retained. Blood oxygen levels are raised about 20% which effectively puts the person at a 20% lower altitude. Nevertheless, it must not be considered a panacea. Climbing too high and too fast, even on Diamox, will lead to mountain sickness and it does have rare side-effects. Any climber must balance the advantages from the drug against its side-effects and obviously its use is a personal choice. Overall, since it dramatically reduces the incidence of mountain sickness, we recommend it for fast ascents at altitudes above 4,000m.

Dr A.R. Bradwell, Senior Lecturer
Birmingham University

MOSQUITO BORNE ILLNESSES

Mosquito borne illnesses are common in the world's tropical areas - Asia, Africa, Mexico, Central and South America, the Caribbean and the South Pacific. And also in not so tropical surrounding areas like the Middle East, Turkey, India, Pakistan, China, Indonesia and North Africa.

The good news for trekkers is that mosquitos don't fly very high and cases of MBIs being contracted above 1,000m are as rare as gnat's teeth. So the time to be vigilant is really when you are in transit en route to the hills and mountains. Take the normal malaria precautions and use insect repellent down low, and you should be fine.

Malaria

Malaria is one of the commonest diseases in the world, caused by the transference of sporozoites of the protozoa "Plasmodium" from infected mosquitos to humans. Malaria destroys the red blood cells, setting off a series of chain reactions which eventually affect the liver and spleen.

Symptoms

Initial symptoms appear six to ten days after being bitten. These are usually low muscular pain and mild fever. Four or so days later the sufferer will have a full fever accompanied by shivering and blue skin, the main characteristics of malaria. These give way to high temperature (up to 107°F

[41.5°C]), headache, delirium, and intense muscular aches. Vomiting and diarrhoea may also be present.

Treatment

Apart from comforting a malaria sufferer and keeping them warm, then cool, as appropriate, they should be given copious amounts of fluid to compensate for fluid loss. This only eases the symptoms - recovery will only happen if Chloroquine based drugs are administered, preferably under the direction of a physician. If medical help is not available then administer Chloroquine. The adult dosage regime for Chloroquine by mouth is: initial dose of 600mg (of base), then a single dose of 300mg after six to eight hours, then a single dose of 300mg daily for two days.

Prevention

Chloroquine can be taken in a 300mg dose (as base) once weekly as prophylaxis backed up with "Paludrine" (Proguanil) in 200mg taken once daily. As there are at least four strains of malaria, some of them resistant to Chloroquine, it is essential to check with your GP before going to Trekland. It has to be taken two weeks prior to departure, and four to six weeks after returning. Side-effects can be numerous - nausea, light-headache, tiredness and loss of appetite being the most common. I have witnessed trekkers who have almost ground to a halt, springing back to rude health only (and almost immediately) after they have stopped taking their daily Paludrine. This seems to be exaggerated above 12,000ft. This doesn't seem to be recognised in the medical world - a little research project there for someone.

Denge fever ("Breakbone Fever")
Denge fever is a mosquito borne viral disease. The secondary symptoms of Denge fever are common to malaria - nausea, chills, fever and muscular aches. However, the initial symptoms are that of flu or hepatitis. The last symptoms, pain in the limbs and joints, end the comparison. The pain seems to run down the length of the bones, the thighs in particular, giving the fever its alternative name. There is no prevention other than using insect repellant, and there is no known cure. But it does pass in ten days without apparently any lasting effects. Comfort can be given to sufferers, however, and codeine helps to kill the pain. Fluids lost must be replaced. And that's all there is to it.

Yellow fever
Found mostly in Africa and South America, this virus shows its first symptoms three to six days after being infected (bitten). These are chills, fever, backache and headache. There may be a slight reprieve in the fever after a few days, but it comes back with a vengeance accompanied by nausea, possibly bleeding gums, bloodshot eyes and red tongue, and because it's yellow fever, jaundice.

Mild causes may feel like flu. As yellow fever is a virus little can be done to treat this other than taking fluids, carbohydrates, bed rest and paracetamol or aspirin.

Vaccines are effective and be sure you receive a vaccine certificate as many countries now insist that you have one, especially if you are arriving from South America or Africa.

WATER BORNE DISEASES AND HEPATITIS B

The following is a hotchpotch of the commonest and most dangerous conditions that can be acquired on trek. Most can be prevented through vaccination and few trekkers contract any of these, but they are sadly still very strong throughout the developing and Third World countries, and you must be very, very careful. Some are borne by water contaminated with faeces - a strong reason for sterilising all water and erecting that toilet tent.

Cholera

Cholera has the initial symptoms of bacterial dysentery, but just doesn't know when to stop. After three days or so the symptoms explode leaving the suffer with little or no control over bowel movements or vomiting, nor any warning. Stools become clear containing flecks of mucus, but rarely blood. Dehydration sets in quickly, leaving the suffer gaunt, shrivelled and dry. Although the symptoms of cholera are normally gone within ten days, the ferocity of this infection warrants treatment by intravenous fluids; on occasion sufferers may die within a few hours. The majority on recovery will be left very weak.

Cholera is very contagious but up country, or in areas of good hygiene, very rare. If you are travelling through an area where cholera is, or has been present, become paranoid about hygiene and cross-infection. Immunization is available and recommended.

Hepatitis A

This is a viral infection that affects the liver and in the majority of cases courses through the victim without them even being aware that they have had it. Symptoms of mild cases are loss of appetite, fatigue, mild fever and lassitude. Most cases do not develop beyond this, but those that do witness an intensity of the symptoms combined with jaundice, stomach discomfort, aching joints and limbs. Rarely fatal, hepatitis A cannot be cured by drugs and symptoms can be around for as long as six months.

Immunization was traditionally with immogloblin, not 100% effective with a short protection span. Recently a course of injections has been developed to give a better and longer (ten year) protection, but has to be administered over a few weeks. Check it out with your GP.

Hepatitis B

Hepatitis B is contracted through bodily fluids: intimate person-to-person contact, contaminated blood, contaminated needles, syringes, tattoo needles and ear piercing equipment, and it's with you for life. Hepatitis B shares the same symptoms as hepatitis A but tends to be more severe, leading to serious liver complications.

There is a vaccine available, but it takes six to eight weeks to take effect, and to a degree is pointless because it is so easy to avoid contracting it. The girls I met in India who had had their ears and noses pierced in Bombay obviously hadn't seen anyone with hepatitis B. Nasty.

Typhoid

Typhoid is an extreme salmonella. For a week after the symptoms appear sufferers complain of fever, headaches and abdominal pain. In the second week a clustered rash appears and the fever increases, often to about 104°F (40°C). The third week brings on confusion, toxic poisoning and green diarrhoea. The fourth week is critical. It can be treated with intravenous antibiotics, but must be diagnosed in time (second week).

Prevention by immunization is not 100% effective, but those who have been immunised and contracted the disease seem to do so at a less acute level, and are not so susceptible to the associated infections and complications synonymous with typhoid.

Diphtheria

Having been under control for decades in the West through immunization, diphtheria is once again on the rise. The collapse of the former Soviet Union, and its immunization programme has seen it creep back towards the developed nations. In tropical countries it has always been present, particularly in the crowded areas with poor sanitation. If you were not immunised as a child then it is possible to be immunised as an adult.

Guinea worm

This is the one that will force you to treat all water. Guinea worm is a water-born parasite that lodges in the stomach or intestine. The dormant larvae is freed by one's digestive juices and over the course of the next 9 to 14 months, the female lays eggs and then starts to burrow out - usually through the legs.

A weal appears just before the worm's head does. You can't pull it out because if it breaks you are very susceptible to infection. Drugs will speed its exit but it may take some time as they can grow up to 2ft long....

Best just purifying the water.

Guinea worm is found in all the places you'll find mosquitos - see Malaria.

OTHER RELATED MEDICAL PROBLEMS
Leeches
A world-wide but fairly harmless problem. Prevalent in jungles and tropical forests, particularly after the monsoon. They have a painless bite, and often the victim is only aware that they have been leeched when they see the blood coming from the wound - long after the leech has had his meal and dropped off.

To remove leeches sprinkle them with salt, lemon juice, insect repellent or vinegar. Don't try and pull them off or you'll develop a sore. Don't try and burn them off or you'll burn your skin!

Prevention is difficult. Cover the skin, particularly the lower legs - gaiters help here. I say prevention is difficult because many of them are tiny, capable of crawling through the lace-holes in boots, or even through the weave of the cloth, in fabric boots. "African Queen" size leeches are not such a problem - you can see them a mile off. It's the ones you can't see... In extreme cases I have witnessed trekkers ring their tent with salt. The worst thing about leeches is the paranoia they induce. Some people recommend insect repellent: my own feeling is that you would have to bathe in the stuff for it to be of any use. They are part of the adventure - so just get on with it!

(*Ed:* Shredded tobacco in socks, under armpits etc. can be an effective deterent.)

Fleas
Fleas are commonly found in the blankets, bedding and carpets of the cutest ethnic houses, and are there to plague patronising, intrusive tourists. Unfortunately, the fleas don't know this and will latch on to anyone who comes within striking distance. They leave small red marks where they have bitten, usually around the waist and armpits or up the legs where they have come up off the carpet. And they itch like crazy.

The cure is to evict the beggars - if possible wash your clothes and yourself, then dust down with flea powder. Scratching the bites will only lead to infection. If it is not possible to wash your clothes then at least turn them inside out and air them well - check the seams for residents. Fleas apparently don't like extremes of heat, so bake or freeze your clothes and sleeping bag when you air them.

Lice
Head lice, I am assured, like clean hair and to lay their little white eggs in the fine hair around the base of the hairline at the neck and ears. Trekkers have the problem with it, not usually the locals, who examine each others heads openly and without stigma, but are happy to pass lice on to anyone.

Treatment is simple - wash hair with anti-lice shampoo, or comb out with a fine tooth comb, or both. Use the shampoo if you have it.

Gynaecological problems
Dysmenorrhoea (period pains)
It is unusual for sufferers to experience this for the first time in the mountains, and should you be prone to menstruation pains make sure you take your usual medication on trek with you - and your hot water bottle. Use aspirin or codeine every 4 hours if you're without your usual preparation.

Cystitis
Cystitis is an infection of the urinary tract which leads to pain when urinating and is accompanied by the feeling that you need to urinate frequently. Predominantly a female problem, and very, very uncomfortable, not to say inconvenient. This is best treated immediately with copious amounts of fluids. Avoid fruit juice (acidic), tea and coffee (stimulants) and favour barley water (alkaline). Consider a course of treatments readily available from your chemist, eg. Cystemme. If the condition persists after two days continue with the fluids and treat with Amoxycillin, 3 times daily for a week.

Thrush
A fungal infection, in this case likely to have been brought on by taking antibiotics, which causes irritation of the vagina and a heavy white discharge. Treat with Canesten cream (Clotrimazole), a fungicide, applied twice a day.

Contraception
By far the biggest weakness of oral contraceptives is their susceptibility to antibiotics which severely reduces their effectiveness. They are also only effective whilst present inside you and thus contraceptive protection cannot be relied upon if sickness and diarrhoea strikes.

Should this problem arise then keep taking the pill to maintain a regular menstrual cycle, but use an alternative contraceptive precaution. Like separate tents. Or camp at 8,000m.

Prolonged use of the contraceptive pill has been proved to increase the chance of the user suffering venous thrombosis, which can develop into a pulmonary embolism. So can spending prolonged periods at altitude and it doesn't take a MENSA quiz setter to realise that participating in both is pushing up the odds a bit. So as a safeguard it would be best to come off the pill at least a month prior to going above 12,000ft. Give yourself a couple of months to allow your menstrual cycle to settle down and to adjust to a comfortable non-oral contraceptive (if required).

Lower altitude treks should present no problem as regards continued use of oral contraceptives, but take an extra month's supply - that late plane could see you late too. Watch when crossing international time boundaries - it may be necessary to move your usual pill-taking time. This being the case consult your GP or local family planning clinic before leaving to avoid a break in cover.

Asthma

Altitude will be less likely to promote an asthma attack than dusty tracks or big hairy yaks. Vic Saunders is an asthmatic and reckons because asthmatics are used to less oxygen they acclimatise quicker and better. If you are asthmatic make sure you have double your usual medication with you, and ask your GP to prescribe you a strong steroid-based back-up in case you have a particularly bad attack out in Trekland.

Gravel rash

This is a nasty but all too common complaint occurring when staggering out of tea houses or slipping on dry glaciers. The cause is irrelevant, the treatment is universal. It is necessary to clean any grit or other particles out of the skin to prevent infection and this is best done with a nail brush and mild antiseptic, after the skin has been anaesthetised. Rub on lignacaine gel to do this.

This can be a rather traumatic experience and it's best if the sufferer cannot witness the clean-up operation. The clean wound should then be dressed after being smeared with an antiseptic cream.

Oral problems

Going off to Trekland without having had a full dental examination beforehand is a form of madness without equal. Problems do arise, if not within your group of trekkers then with the boys within your service crew and the more often one goes up high, the greater the odds of having these problems. It seems that the problems stem from air trapped within fillings, which is subject to expansion and contraction at altitude. The filling becomes lose, with older metal-based fillings being particularly prone to this. Even if the filling remains within its cavity, because it has been loosened it allows air into the tooth, increasing the risk of infection and pain, weakens it with the possibility of breaking, or worse still, the filling may come out altogether.

Closely associated with toothache are gum infections, abscesses or boils. And if that lot isn't enough add tongue and gum ulcers just to completely spoil your appetite. And your trek.

There are several emergency dental kits on the market at the moment, all of which seem perfect for the job, though these are added expense when all that is needed are a few additions to the medical kit. A small examination mirror, used in conjunction with a head torch, usually is all that is needed to pinpoint the problem, and a small amount of zinc-oxide compound will form a temporary filling - pushed into the cavity with a sterile probe or cotton bud. Zinc-oxide compounds are not made from zinc-oxide tape! It is a paste that hardens when exposed to moisture - in this case saliva. Cavit and Cimpast are two brand names, and your friendly dentist will give you half a film container's worth if you show them a nice smile, brush three times a day and visit him every six months. Which of course you do anyway...

For toothache you can't go far wrong with good old-fashioned oil of cloves. Dabbed on the sore spot with a pad of cotton wool or cotton bud it is pretty effective, and can be used with other low grade painkillers such as codeine or aspirin. Infections of the gum are best treated with a broad spectrum antibiotic such as Amoxycillin: 250mg 3 times daily for 5 days.

Boils can be lanced (drained) by trained dental personnel using one of your own sterile needles and syringes. Trained personnel only though - it takes a long time and a lot of work to become a dentist, and for good reason.

Ulcers can be effectively covered with a proprietary oral balm such as Bonjela. Don't be tempted to use Zylocanie gel, or similar, as this is definitely poisonous if taken internally.

Where there is a thriving expat. community there will be a dentist to serve it, and if you are having problems a call to the Embassy - British, Australian, NZ, or American - will usually supply you with the name of a dentist to help you out. Ditto the above for doctors.

On no account go to a local quack. Whilst they may display with pride the results of their quick and public extractions, they do not indicate how many of their previous clients succumbed to serious post-extraction infections, or the number of their clients who left in appalling pain because of careless operations.

FIRST-AID KITS
Personal
The following is a suggestion for a small personal first-aid kit suitable for carrying in your rucksack for use on a day-to-day basis, and designed to complement your group's main medicine chest.

1	x	antiseptic cream (small)
2	x	sterile dressings
1	x	crepe bandage (4mm)
1	x	eye patch
10	x	adhesive plasters or 1 adhesive plaster strip
1	x	zinc-oxide tape

1   x   strip of moleskin or second skin
1   x   triangular bandage (or use your neckerchief...)
Small bottle of tincture of iodine
4   x   butterfly stitches (dumbell stitches)
12   safety pins
4   x   pieces of Melolin
12   x   aspirin
12   x   throat lozenges
6   x   Imodium or Lomotil
12   x   sachets ORS
1   x   tube of eye ointment
1   x   tweezers
1   x   scissors

Keep a suitable supply of spares - lozenges, aspirin, plasters etc. - in your kit bag to allow a restock. In addition, the following drugs won't go amiss, either for personal use or as a back-up for the main medicine chest. Keep wrapped in polythene in your kit bag.

20   x   Diamox (if appropriate)
20   x   Ciproxin (or general broad-spectrum antibiotic)
12   x   Fasigyn (or Metronidazole)
12   x   Trimethoprim (dose 200mg 2 times daily for 5-7 days)
30   x   aspirin

It would appear that all that's missing from this list is a pair of delivery forceps and a green boiler suit. Whilst this may resemble a paramedic's tool kit, it is not as bulky or as extensive as you might think, and can easily be contained in a small toilet bag. In fact a small waterproof toilet bag makes an ideal first-aid container. So also do 1 litre waterproof polythene kitchen containers - particularly handy if used on board boats or canoes.

Commercially available first-aid kits vary so much in quality and content, have a tendency to be aimed at car and home use, and are too bulky to be of much use to the trekker. Those aimed at hill-walkers and mountaineers are often very attractively packaged but contain little and will need to be supplemented to cover potential trekking problems, so I strongly advise making up your own. Buy in bulk to make up two or three kits and split the costs with friends.

I feel that everyone should carry a small kit, even if you are a member of a large party, as you inevitably end up administering to the service crew or local people and one kit can be plundered very quickly. If the thought of even sticking a plaster on a small cut is making you giddy, or if your knowledge of first-aid is so poor that you think ABC are only the first letters of the alphabet, then carry a first-aid kit - the person next to you may be a brain surgeon, or better still a first-aider.

If travelling closely in a small group, eg. roped up across a glacier, or on summit day, then one kit each may seem excessive and one between the group will suffice. Check to make sure someone is carrying it though!

Group First-Aid/Medicine Chest (FAMCh)
Every group needs a communal first-aid/medicine chest for themselves and their crew. It is very important that it is administered very carefully to prevent misuse or theft. No use opening up the box to discover Jim has used all the antibiotics on the yak with a cough, or that the cook has bound all the beef-olives together with the dumb-bell sutures. Ideally it should be the responsibility of a single person, who reports back to the others on its status. On commercial trips give this responsibility to the WTL. Around camp it should be kept in a prominent position, usually in the mess tent, where it is known to be available in case of emergency, but in a non-emergency opened only by its custodian. Locking it is not advisable. At night, for security, it can live under someone's fly sheet, as long as the whole company knows whose tent.

En route, the FAMCh should be accessible - preferably carried by the rear marker, who is usually one of the sirdars' assistants. Remember, trouble comes to the back - often it is difficult to send forward for something, but it is easy to wait for the rear to catch up, so keep the FAMCh there.

The FAMCh is no doubt bulky and susceptible to moisture, so a proper container is essential for it. Small 10 litre barrels (referred to as pickle barrels in the USA) can be pressed into service - especially good if it's going to be a very wet trip - as can ex-army ammunition boxes. But the former tend to have poor access and the latter tend to be heavy, and both are awkward shapes. Still an awkward shape but a good compromise is a single compartment, heavy polythene, tool box. Readily available in car accessory shops, ironmongers and Woolworths. The quality of these boxes varies enormously and this is usually reflected in the price. Most have a removable tray inside, which is very convenient, but this can be substituted with margarine or ice-cream containers. Weak areas are the hinges and the clasps/locks. Good quality ones will have a seal between the base and the lid. Obviously best bought in the UK. Divide the contents of the FAMCh under headings, as stated in the list later, wrapped in polythene or in waterproof containers.

Drugs prescribed in bubble packs have a tendency to pop out of their wrappers, and this can be prevented by taping over them with parcel tape or zinc-oxide tape. Write the details of the drugs in indelible ink on the tape. A copy of the *British National Formula* (BNF) or a *MIMS* (Monthly Index of Medical Specialities) is a good addition to the box. Both these publications list drugs by their proprietary and generic names and give the usual dose, list any side-effects, drugs they should not be used alongside, precautions etc. Not on sale to the general public but available via sympathetic pharmacists and GPs (But don't say I said so.) A full contents list should also be enclosed and a list, kept in a sealed envelope (or with the WTL where appropriate), of the medical details of the expedition members, including any known allergies and blood types.

Finally, enclose small note book and pen to list any contents used, and also to record details of drugs administered to patients and other relevant details - time administered, dosage, pulse, general conditions, etc.

Drugs and medical equipment are very expensive in the UK but extremely cheap in South America and Asia, and there is a very strong case for buying out there - like saving £900 on a 10 person medical kit.

Quality control, or lack of it, has given third world produced drugs a bad reputation, not altogether deserved, for being "watered down". However, all the medical centres I've witnessed run by westerners in the third world have administered locally (!) made drugs to apparently good effect. If it's good enough for them then it's good enough for me, and I personally have never experienced or heard of problems with Sub European Drugs.

If in doubt as to whether the drugs/equipment you need are available in Trekland, ask one of the commercial operators. Don't ask the consuls - if unavailable they are likely to be too embarrassed to admit it.

Returning home with such a box of heinous chemicals may raise a few eyebrows at customs - a letter from your GP stating your role as medical officer on your trip, if she/he is agreeable, can help. Better still is having a detailed knowledge of its contents to impress the officers, which of course you should have. Or you could thank all the locals who make your trip so good by giving the lot away to the local health post or hospital at the end of your trek. No problems with customs then. Anyway, here is a basic 10-15 person FAMCh, with a basic description of each drug. Keep a copy of it in your big box together with the quantities list.

Analgesics

CODEINE PHOSPHATE - Dose 15mg. A stronger painkiller than Paracetamol, dose 1-2 tabs every 4-6 hours.

PARACETAMOL - 500mg tabs. Dose 2 tabs every 4-6 hours for mild pain.

DIHYDROCODEINE (DF 118) - 30mg tabs. Dose 1-2 tabs every 4-6 hours for moderate pain. May cause constipation with prolonged use.

BUPRENORPHINE (TEMGESIC) - 0-2mg tabs. Dose 1-2 tabs dissolved under the tongue for SEVERE pain. BUPRENORPHINE IS A POWERFUL OPIATE ANALGESIC RELATED TO MORPHINE. Unlike morphine, it can be taken by mouth (dissolved under the tongue). It is a controlled drug and must be used with care. Its most dangerous side-effect is respiratory depression (ie. it may cause breathing difficulties). It must therefore be used with great care in anyone who already has breathing problems, eg. chest injuries (rib fractures, pneumothorax) or pulmonary edema (altitude sickness).

Anti-Inflammatories
These drugs are useful in the treatment of fractures and soft tissue injuries (eg. sprained ankles, bad backs, etc.). They reduce swelling and inflammation, and also have some analgesic effect. They should not be given to those with stomach ulcers or bad indigestion.

IBUPROFEN (BRUGEN) - 200mg tabs. Dose 2-3 tabs 3 times a day. Useful for joint/muscle pain related to sprains, fractures, etc. Should be taken after food as it may cause stomach upsets.

MEFENAMIC ACID (PONSTAN) - 250mg tabs. Dose 2 tabs 3 times a day. A more powerful drug than Ibruprofen for more severe injuries. It is more likely to cause stomach upsets and should also be taken with food. It is VERY good for bad backs in conjunction with Methocarbamol. Also very good for period pains (Dysmenorrhoea). This must not be taken if diarrhoea persists as it can go on to cause dehydration and kidney failure.

Antibiotics
These are anti-bacterial drugs used in the treatment of infection. REMEMBER that all drugs ending in "-cillin" are penicillin derivatives, therefore ALWAYS ask your patient if he is allergic to penicillin before prescribing. If he/she is, use an alternative drug.

FASIGYN (Tinidazole), brand name Tinibar - 500mg seems preferred and probably more practical treatment in Asia for amoebic dysentery or Gardia. 2gm (4 x 500mg) once a day for 2-3 days complete the course.

AMOXYCILLIN (AMOXIL) - 250mg tabs. Dose 2 tabs 3 times a day or AMPICILLIN (PENBRITIN) - 500mg tabs. Dose 1 tab 4 times a day.
Used for tonsillitis, sinusitis, chest infection, urinary tract infection, otitis media (middle ear infection) and tooth abscess (with Metronidazole). Severe infections such as pneumonia will require an intravenous injection of 500mg dissolved in sterile water 3 or 4 times a day.

FLUCLOXACILLIN (FLOXAPEN) - 250mg tabs. Dose 2 tabs 4 times a day. Used for skin infection (cellulitis, impetigo, etc.), wound infections, abscesses. Severe skin infections will require an intravenous injection of 500mg 4 times a day. For compound fractures intravenous Flucloxacillin (500mg 4 times a day) and intravenous Amoxycillin/Ampicillin are given to prevent serious bone infection.

ERYTHROMYCIN - 250mg tabs. Dose 2 tabs 4 times a day. A useful alternative to penicillin drugs for chest, skin and wound infection in people who are allergic to penicillin. Should also be used for chest infections which fail to improve after a few days of Amoxycillin.

METRONIDAZOLE (FLAGYL) - 400mg tabs. Dose 1 tab 3 times a day. Used for dental abscess (with Ampicillin), vaginitis, amoebic dysentery (double the dose to 2 tabs 3 times a day). For peritonitis (due to penetrating wounds to the abdomen, perforated ulcer, burst appendix, etc.) intravenous injection of 500mg 3 times a day is given with intravenous Gentamicin. Also traditional treatment for amoebic dysentery and Giardia.

COTRIMOXAZOLE (SEPTRIN) - 960mg tabs. Dose 1 tab twice a day. Is like Trimethoprim used for urine infections (cystitis) and chest infections. However it may cause skin rashes and rarely blood disorders. Also traditional treatment for bacillary dysentery and can treat typhoid.

CHLORAMPHENICOL EYE DROPS OR OINTMENT (CHLOROMYCETIN) - Dose 2 drops every 3 hours or ointment 4 times a day. For conjunctivitis.

OTOSPORIN EAR DROPS - Dose 3 drops 4 times a day. For otitis external (outer ear canal infection).

ACYCLOVIR CREAM (ZOVIRAX) - Dose apply 4-5 times daily. For cold sores and other herpes simplex infections.

CIPROFLOXACIN (CIPROXIN) - 250mg, NORFLOXACIN (NEGAFLOX) - 400mg, OFLOXACIN (TARIVID) - 400mg.
All similar new generation antibiotic. Preferred treatment in SE Asia for bacillary dysentery. Dosage 1 tab 4 times a day for 5 days. Also a typhoid treatment but take 10-14 days. Take 2 hours after eating, NOT with indigestion remedies.

Antihistamines

For the treatment of allergic reactions.

ANTIHISTAMINE CREAM - Dose apply 3 times a day. For insect bites, poison ivy, nettle rash, etc. Relieves itching, reduces swelling.

PIRITON TABS (CHLORPHENIRAMINE) - 4mg. 1 tab 3-4 times a day. Will cause drowsiness.

Diarrhoea

LOPERAMIDE HYDROCHLORIDE (IMODIUM) - 2mg capsules. Dose initially 2 caps then 1 cap after every bowel movement, maximum 16mg daily.

DIOCALM (Boots) - for mild diarrhoea.

DIORALYTE (ORS) - Dose 1 sachet in a glass of water. Replaces salt and minerals lost in diarrhoea. You can safely consume as much Dioralyte as you can with no risk of overdose. Around 6 sachets a day is usually

sufficient, but you may reach 8-16 sachets a day if you rely on it for total fluid replacement (16 sachets = 4 litres).
AIM TO DRINK 4-5 LITRES OF WATER A DAY.

Altitude (Mountain) Sickness

ACETAZOLAMIDE (DIAMOX) - 250mg tabs. Dose initially 2 tabs then 1 tab 2 times a day. Useful for mild altitude sickness.

ASPIRIN (SALICYLIC ACID) - 300mg tabs. Dose 1 tab a day. Aspirin should ALWAYS be given for symptoms of altitude sickness. At this dose it reduces the risk of venous thrombosis (blood clots) in the extremities and pulmonary emboli (blood clots on the lungs) which can be fatal.

FRUSEMIDE (LASIX) - 40mg tabs. Lasix is used to treat pulmonary edema which has been caused by heart related illness. Symptoms are shortness of breath, especially when lying flat, rarely frothing at the mouth. Current medical opinion suggests it has little effect on high altitude pulmonary edema. Dose 1 tab initially. If no improvement, 2 tabs after 4 hours. The dose can be increased to 4 tabs daily. Used for pulmonary edema. RAPID DESCENT IS THE MOST IMPORTANT TREATMENT FOR PULMONARY EDEMA.

DEXAMETHASONE - 2mg tabs. Dose 2 tabs 4 times a day. Used for cerebral edema in conjunction with rapid descent. Symptoms are drowsiness, lack of co-ordination, high pulse rate at rest, irritability, convulsions, coma and death. Provided this drug has been administered for a short period of time (less than 5 days) it may be stopped suddenly. If used for longer periods it must be gradually reduced under medical supervision.

NIFEDIPINE - Used for pulmonary edema in conjunction with rapid descent. Dose initially 10mg. If no improvement another 10mg, 2 hours later, then 5 to 20mg per day until condition stabilises. If immediate effect is required, bite capsule and let liquid stay in the mouth.

Miscellaneous

VENTOLIN INHALER (SALBUTAMOL) - For asthma type conditions. 2 puffs 4 times daily.

METOCLORPRAMIDE (MAXOLON) - 10mg tabs. Dose 1 tab every 8 hours. (Avoid administering to those under 20 years old.) For nausea and vomiting.

PROCHLORPERAZINE (STEMETIL) - 5mg tabs. Dose 1 tab 3 times a day. For severe nausea and vomiting, severe dizziness, motion sickness, labyrinthine disorders (labyrinthitis, Meniere's disease).

AMETHOCAINE - 0.5ml sachets. Dose 1 sachet. Local anaesthetic drugs applied to the eye. Used for extracting foreign bodies from the eye. AN EYE PATCH MUST BE WORN FOR 12 HOURS TO PREVENT ACCIDENTAL

DAMAGE TO THE ANAESTHETISED EYE IF AMETHOCAINE IS USED.

FLUOURESCEIN SODIUM DROPS - 1-2% sachets. Dose 1 sachet. A fluorescent dye applied to the eye in order to show up foreign bodies (eg. splinters, grit).

INDIGESTION TABLETS - Dose suck/chew 1-2 tabs as required. For indigestion.

XYLOCAINE CREAM - 25g tube. Dose apply mornings and night after defecation for haemorrhoids. Also useful as local anaesthetic on skin when cleaning up small grazes or gravel rash.

LIGNOCAINE HYDROCHLORIDE - 2% 50ml bottle. Maximum dose 10ml. Should be plain (ie. not with adrenalin). Local anaesthetic which can be injected under the skin around a wound prior to suturing. Please note that this drug is FATAL if injected into the blood supply. *Medicine for Mountaineering* (see Recommended Reading) now suggests that soft tissue injuries should not be sutured in the field if this can be avoided.

SENOKOT or DULCO-LAX - for constipation.

DEEP HEAT

Drug List

	Dose	Quantity
FASIGYN (TINIBAR)	500mg	20
PARACETAMOL	500mg	25
BUPRENORPHINE (TEMGESIC)	0.2mg	20
IBUPROFEN (BRUFEN)	200mg	30
MEFENAMIC ACID (PONSTAN)	250mg	20
AMOXYCILLIN (AMOXIL)	250mg	40
AMPICILLIN (PENBRITIN)	500mg	40
FLUCLOXACILLIN (FLOXAPEN)	250mg	40
ERYTHROMYCIN	250mg	30
METRONIDAZOLE (FLAGYL)	400mg	40
COTRIMOXAZOLE (SEPTRIN)	500mg	40
CHLORAMPHENICOL DROPS (CHLOROMYCETIN)	10ml	1
OTOSPORIN DROPS	10ml	1
ACYCLOVIR CREAM (ZOVIRAX)	10g	1
ANTIHISTAMINE CREAM	25g	1
PIRITON		20
NIFEDIPINE	5mg	20
ACETAZOLAMIDE (DIAMOX)	250mg	25
SALICYCLIC ACID (ASPIRIN)	300mg	100

	Dose	Quantity
FRUSEMIDE (LASIX)	40mg	20
DEXAMETHASONE	2mg	40
LOPERAMIDE HYDROCHLORIDE (IMODIUM)	2mg	50
DIORALYTE		20
METOCLORPRAMIDE (MAXOLON)	10mg	20
AMETHOCAINE	0.5ml	5
FLUORESCEIN SODIUM DROPS	0.5ml	2
XYLOCAINE CREAM	25g	1
SENNA (SENOKOT)	7.5mg	10
PROCHLORPERAZINE (STEMETIL)	5mg	20
LIGNOCAINE HYDROCHLORIDE 2%	50ml inj	1
ANTISEPTIC CREAM		1
IODINE TINCTURE (2%)		2
THROAT LOZENGES		100
VIC VAPOUR RUB		1
IBUPROFEN CREAM		1
SALBUTAMOL (VENTOLIN INHALER)		1
CANESTEN CREAM		1
CYSTEMME		18 sachets

Medical first-aid kit
Elastoplast: 3 rolls
Assorted plasters: 1 box
Moleskin: 2 sheets
Crepe bandage 2", 3", 4": 1 each
Cotton wool: 1 small pack
Eye pads: 2
Safety pins: 20
Dressing towels (swabs): 5
Triangular bandage: 2
Emergency splint - eg. Sam Splint: 1
No.15 wound dressing: 2
Extra large wound dressing: 1
No.8 lint dressing: 1
Normasol solution: 6
Throat lozenges: 100
Small dressing - eg. Melolin (non-adherent): 12
Large dressing - eg. Melolin (non-adherent): 12

Antibiotic powder: 1
Clingfilm: 4 sheets
Surgical gloves: 2
Disposable gloves: 10
5mm syringes: 4
10mm syringes: 4
Assorted needles: 6
Catgut sutures with cutting needle 2/0: 2
Silk sutures with cutting needle 2/0, 4/0, 6/0: 2 each
Thermometer: 1
Needle holder: 1
Toothed forceps: 1 (for stitching)
Stitch cutting blades: 3
Skin closures: 3 packets (dumb-bell sutures)
Dettol: 1
Scissors: 1

Suggestions for medical kit

1 large pair of scissors for cutting clothing
1 large Venflon for pneumothorax
Use disposable scalpels. They are lighter and more hygenic than handles
with disposable blades
Carry clingfilm for burns
1 butterfly needle - for intravenous drips etc.
1 general-purpose stethoscope.

Sutures

It is important to carry the right size suture on the right needle. For lacerations
on the trunk and limbs, heavy silk sutures size 2/0 are ideal. The needle should
be a large 'cutting' needle, eg. round bodied, atraumatic, are not as good. You
might, therefore, use: 2/0 MERSILK on a 45mm cutting needle.

For lacerations on the face you need fine man-made monofilament sutures
such as Prolene or Ethilon, size 4/0 or 6/0. A small cutting needle this time, eg:
4/0 ETHILON on a 16mm cutting needle.

Catgut sutures are used for internal fat/muscle lacerations before stitching
the skin. Consider using: 2/0 CHROMIC on a 45mm cutting needle.

You will also need to carry a pair of toothed forceps to hold the skin edge.
Also a needle holder. A small pair of artery clips (haemostat) are just as good
but smaller and lighter than needle holders.

Useful addresses
Nomad Travellers Store and Travellers Medical Centre
3 Wellington Terrace
Turnpike Lane
London N8
(0181) 441 7208

UIAA Mountain Medicine Centre
St Bartholomew's Hospital
London
EC1A 7BE

The centre is run on a voluntary basis by Dr Charles Clarke and Mrs Ann Tilley, advising climbers and mountain travellers, as well as expedition doctors, on all aspects of mountain related illnesses.

Information sheets are available on:

1) Mountain sickness, edemas and travel to high altitudes
2) Climbing at extreme altitudes above 7,000m
3) Diamox, Decadron and Nifedipine at high altitudes
4) Portable compression chamber in AMS
5) First-aid kits
6) Sunscreens and altitude
7) International transport of drugs and oxygen from Britain
8) Oxygen systems available for use at altitude
9) Causes of death at extreme altitude
10) Frost-bite - practical suggestions
11) The oral contraceptive pill at high altitude

There is a £2.00 cover charge for each sheet. Available from the above address.

Recommended reading
Medicine for Mountaineering by James Wilkerson (The Mountaineers)
Travellers Health by Richard Darwood (Oxford University Press)
Expedition Medicine by B. Juel-Jenson (Royal Geographical Society)

CHAPTER SIX
Equipment

"Ten coolie loads of baggage and stores should suffice for the single traveller. The regulation load is fifty pounds, so one's impedimenta must be distributed accordingly...a folding chair and table, a portable leather bath, a rifle and a photographic camera formed a portion of my collection of necessaries..."

E.F. Knight, Where 3 Empires Meet *(1891)*

CLOTHING

In the good old days when men were men and women didn't go near mountains, choosing the proper clothes for the mountains was an easy job - wool long johns or combos, followed by a woolly shirt and jersey, topped off by as many layers of tweed as was necessary whilst still being able to bend the appropriate joints to allow walking/climbing. Eventually came oil and its derivatives - fabrics like nylon and Merkalon were quickly utilised by gear manufacturers to create clothing that was designed specifically for the outdoors. A few die-hards retained the old, dismissing the new on the grounds that if it didn't make you scratch, or sag to your knees when wet, then it was useless. Those with more sense, lumbago or an aversion to getting wet saw the light and kitted themselves out in sensible clothes, not caring if it was traditional or not. Now the rise in the number of people enjoying the outdoors has seen the over development of outdoor clothing and equipment almost to the extent where colour and style have taken precedent over practicality. Living in a consumer society does have its advantages, however, and careful choice from the huge selection available today should see you kitted at a reasonable cost.

Whilst the old-timers may have scratched and chafed a bit, their principles were spot on, namely dressing in layers and the use of fabrics that maintain their insulating qualities even when wet, or indeed frozen.

Modern fabrics are hyper-efficient, making the layer system even more effective. Layering works on the principle that each layer traps air between. This trapped air is heated by our bodies and remains warm because of the insulating nature of the fabric. Basic physics that work well. Temperature is controlled by either adding or removing layers to maintain the desired effect. Several thin layers offer more control and are more effective than a few thick layers, and the thin layers available today are works of art. Merkalon and polypropylene thermal underwear not only trap air and keep it warm, but they also allow sweat to be whisked away from the body to keep it dry. Bodies are less prone to sweat rash and, more importantly, don't chill so quickly. Wet clothing sticks to the body and in the wind cools the body down. More basic physics, but not always obvious. This is one reason why cotton is not so good, because it absorbs and retains so much moisture.

Trekking takes place from the high, cold mountain regions to the desert and, as such, is subject to the extremes of temperatures that occur there, from intense cold to extreme heat and everything in between, often in the space of a day. Layering (or having thirty porters carrying all your different outfits so you can change every hour) is the only solution. We'll start by covering our own layer of breathable fabric - our skin.

The first layer should be of aforementioned Merkalon or polypropylene, and should consist of long johns and a long-sleeved vest. You don't really want a polo neck at this stage but a round neck. The long sleeves offer your arms protection from the sun and can be made shorter by rolling them up... or if you don't need them or can't get on with them, cut them off. However, if your limbs are well insulated then you save energy when the temperature drops by making it easier for your body to keep you warm.

There are several different weights of 'thermals' (a term used to describe a garment worn next to the skin) and the one chosen depends on where it's to be used. If in doubt stick to a medium weight, although if you are going up high (above the snowline) for a long time, or it will be used in the winter time, then opt for a thicker type. Thin thermals fit nicely under everyday clothes and are great for extreme Christmas shopping trips. All thermals make great pyjamas, which you will want to wear after you've read the section on sleeping bags. Often this is all you'll need for a day with only a T-shirt and shorts over the top - the Antipodean look (also favoured by North Americans). (I believe the idea of shorts is to protect one's modesty as thermals do tend to follow the body contours very closely. Also being thin, thermals are irresistible to abrasive surfaces...)

After the thermals comes an intermediate layer over the core - the area most precious as it contains our vital organs - and this is simply a good old-fashioned shirt or a complicated state-of-the-art shirt. Regardless of your choice, in style or material, it should have ventilation round the neck and a collar that can be turned up. For an isolated day on the hill my favourite is a silk lined, Virginia wool, buttoned down the front, chest pocket lumber jacket shirt, but for continual use a thick polypropylene, zip neck polo which is more practical, being quicker to dry (and wash) and easier to scrunch up into a rucksack or kit bag. For intermediate wear on the legs how about a pair of trousers? Or a trekking skirt for the ladies? We are looking at a medium-weight material for both garments, like a durable cotton, but preferably a cotton polyester mix. Trousers should be of a loose cut, preferably with a reinforced seat, and have good pockets, one of which should have a zipper. Rohan started the trend with their 'bags' but there are lots of makes and models of that ilk. The choice is yours.

The trekking skirt is not just me being silly: I have seen many women wearing them on trek and those I have spoken to deem them to be very comfortable and practical as long as there is no need to wear a harness or climb or scramble over rocks or wade through rivers. Also modesty is preserved on the Great Open Plains when nature calls.

Over this goes a pile suit - a jacket and trousers as opposed to a one-piece. I suggest having zipped pockets in both these garments, as the nature of pile fabric makes for very loose and floppy pockets which tend to eject Mars bars and Swiss army knives, just before you need them. A high collar on the jacket helps keep the ears warm when the evening wind gets up.

WATERPROOFS

The final layer should be a wind and waterproof shell. "Breathable" fabrics are the thing nowadays. Most work on the simple principle of allowing warm water vapour (ie. sweat) out, and preventing cold rain from getting in. This transpiration requires space, so regardless of quality, if the garment is too tight a fit it's not going to "breathe". Likewise, where it's compressed onto the next layer, ie. under rucksack straps or on the back. Dirt delays the process too, so shells made from these materials should be kept clean. Also, breathable fabrics can only breath at a certain rate - the equivalent to an English summer rainstorm. As soon as you move up to Scottish West Highland autumn deluge then it starts running out of breath. By the time you've reached Delhi in the monsoon it's beginning to look as if it's got bronchitis, smokes and works down the mine.

The alternatives are even worse. Polyurethane proofed nylon, which leaves you soaked in your own condensed perspiration, or waxed cotton, which whilst being pretty effective against the elements is too heavy to be practical on trek.

The cut and style of your shell must take into account the amount of clothing that you may be wearing under it, and the fact that it does need to breathe. Jackets should have a two-way zip and stud fastening down the front to offer ventilation in less extreme weather. Be wary of too much Velcro as this tends to ball up with pile, or gum up with snow and ice. Quite a few jackets on the market have "pit-zips" under the arms to increase ventilation, but having spoken to the owners of several models with this feature, the consensus is that they merely allow water another entrance, rather than an exit.

Hoods should be BIG to give helmets, woolly hats and dreadlocks room, and with either a wire or a drawstring round the edge to allow it to be closed over the face, stop it flapping and protect your face.

Pockets are better being the kind that are sewn onto the outside of the jacket rather than inserted, as this leaves the fabric of the jacket punctured only by the sewing machine rather than a gaping hole. Pockets should also have flaps over them, hindering water seepage. How many pockets is up to yourself, but a map pocket, inserted beside the zip and the garment and not puncturing the main jacket, is very handy for maps, wallets, dog biscuits etc. If you do have a map pocket sew a little tab inside to tie your compass to. Pockets lower down are great for keeping hands and gloves in, but can be a nuisance when putting on harnesses. Unless you are wearing a full body harness, in which case ALL pockets will get in the way.... Finally, ALL materials should have seams taped on the reverse to keep them waterproof. If you count the panels on some jackets and look underneath you'll see that the way they are assembled doesn't allow all the seams to be taped. It also makes sense that the more seams there are, the greater the chance of a leak.

Whether you have lined waterproofs is up to yourself - they do have a nice feel when dry and add little to the weight. They are the opposite when wet, however, and don't allow you to examine the underside properly. A jacket that reaches down over the hips sheds water and wind off your sensitive bits and onto the top of your legs, although it doesn't matter much if you are wearing a good pair of water and windproof trousers. The same maxims apply as regard materials and construction. The cut here is important. First of all, get trousers that have zips up the leg, at least to the knee, to facilitate fitting and removal whilst still wearing your boots. All the way to the hip allows you to go to the loo without removing them. Two definite bonuses above the snowline in the extreme cold. Another important feature is to make sure that they are a nice snug fit below the knee to prevent you snagging them with your crampons.

Make sure that the trousers come high at the back to keep your kidneys and lower back warm and dry.

Keep water/snow/dust and mud out of your boots with a pair of gaiters. These should again be zipped to allow fitting without removing your boot, and once more should be as snug a fitting as the trousers because of crampons.

As with any piece of shell clothing, the heavier the weight of material they are made from, the more effective and harder wearing they are going to be at the cost of price and weight.

OTHER BITS

Even with all this, there are still a few bits sticking out that are going to get cold. Well, if you want to get ahead - get a hat. Several in fact. For the sunshine, you need something to keep the sun off your neck and shade your face, and even stop your ears getting burnt. Big floppy cotton sun hats are cheap and effective. An alternative with more nose/eye protection is a baseball cap. Sew a handkerchief on the back to protect your neck. It doesn't do much for your ears though.

In the cold, a hat is going to reduce heat loss by an astounding 25-40%. It takes energy to create heat, so by wearing a hat you are saving energy. Saving energy becomes a priority at altitude, and you must wear a hat at all times. Buy a good fleece-lined hat with ear protection, a skip, a chin strap and a windproof/waterproof outer covering. You might also buy a good old-fashioned Balaclava to compliment it - very sensible, but don't buy one made from itchy wool!

Don't forget your digits. If you want to boost the heating in the fingers and toes department then pop on an extra jumper. When you start to get cold your body starts to prioritise about what to do with the available heat. As all our vital organs are kept in our trunk, then it gets first shout for warmth. Toes and fingers are pretty low on the list. Even with a warm core the extremities do get cold in the snow and the wind. So let's have a look at what's on offer.

Mitts have become very unpopular due mainly to the fact that anyone wearing them looks like a six-year-old on their way to school. In many respects they shouldn't be overlooked, because unless manipulation is a priority, mitts can be very warm and extremely comfortable. A badly fitting glove, on the other hand, can cause circulation problems in the fingers and defeat their purpose.

Regardless of whether you go for gloves or mitts, fit elastic wrist loops to them to stop you dropping them or leaving them behind - not too long or they'll get in the way when your gloves are off.

Gloves follow the layer system already discussed. The first layer should be the thinnest and made from Merkalon. Being so thin and next to the skin allows the wearer to use cameras and other bits of fiddly gear without either sticking to it (extremely cold) or losing all feeling. Being very light and compact means they blow away easily and get lost as soon as you take your gaze off them. So always have two pairs on trek. They are useless when wet also, unless they have a layer over them. Enter the next layer.

Again, you choose. You can either dispense with the inner gloves and go for a ski-type glove or add to them with another layer. Ski gloves, I think, are good for a day, but despite being made from the most up-to-date materials most of them need drying out every evening because they retain sweat, or let in moisture - the seams are purely for fashion. They do have a very comfortable cosiness about them and usually have good leather palms to help you when you're scrambling about. For sustained use, where you may have to put the gloves on damp or even wet, go for either fibre pile, or more traditional wool.

Fibre pile is fine - just make sure the fingers aren't too tight or too short and that the cuff comes up well over the wrist. Wool gloves for the outdoors should be a bit more substantial than the ones your granny knits everyone for Christmas. The wool should be oiled for a start - not as desperate as it sounds. And the finished product should have been shrunk, also ensuring that it is very close knit. The closer the knit the warmer and more water-resistant the product will be. Both fleece and wool develop a frozen shell over them in extreme conditions, taking on the appearance of body armour, but keeping out the elements to good effect and keeping in the heat.

Prolonged use in snowy, wet conditions, or use at altitude, is going to necessitate another layer - an outer waterproof/windproof glove or mitt, fleecy lined if conditions dictate. Make sure they have an elasticated wrist and come up over your jacket cuff. And there you have it, the complete Michelin Man outfit! Apart from the duvet jacket. If you are going to be up high and/ or in the cold then a good down duvet jacket is going to raise your comfort factor considerably. Usually they are too warm to work in and are thus a camp luxury, making life after sun down practical and enjoyable. It's the difference between sitting watching the sun set and moon rise and trying to keep warm in a featureless tent. Until the down gets wet, of course, when you have a bag of wet feathers. Care instructions as for a sleeping bag. A number of duvet jackets on the market have a breathable fabric shell. Very nice if you can afford them.

If it's a real holiday then you'll want some T-shirts and shorts, just to let the air and sun in about you for an hour or so. Running shorts may be light, but tend to do little for modesty (see "attitudes" later on): best keep them baggy with a pocket here or there.

T-shirts should be baggy too - sweaty, tight T-shirts cling, becoming very unpleasant. Avoid potentially offensive designs and avoid white! The best of efforts on trek are unlikely to keep a white shirt white for long. Black is where it's at. Two T-shirts are enough - wear one, wash the other. Give or throw them away at the end of trek.

You may find the clothing check list at the end of this section useful when packing.

BOOTS/FOOTWARE

If any item of kit needs to be just right before you go out, then it has to be your boots. Other gear can be borrowed, adapted or replaced but not your boots. If you ruin your feet on trek you've blown your chances of success, unless you are very, very lucky. A strong heart and lungs won't propel you up your chosen path without the full cooperation of your feet and whilst pain and discomfort in almost every other department can be masked to a point, throbbing feet and ankles cannot....

Before buying boots consider what they are to be used for, and under what conditions. Also have a look at yourself - are you experienced, light and dainty on your feet, or perhaps a little overweight or a little clumsy? All these things will have some bearing on your choice of boot. Remember that when you are walking, the weight and forces involved in this activity are borne by your joints, particularly your hips, knees and ankles. A good pair of boots will alleviate these stresses, support and help protect them.

You wouldn't think that socks and insoles would make much difference to how you walk, but once again the space programme has produced new materials that make you wonder how we ever managed before. If you are anything other than the average British size and shape, then first consideration is a pair of Sorbothane insoles. Give them two weeks and you'll not only notice the difference on the soles of your feet but also your knees. Clever stuff, the key being that the foam rubber has bubbles of nitrogen as opposed to oxygen inside it. This stops it collapsing, apparently.

If you have other than an average foot that may need extra support, then you'll need to have insoles moulded to your feet. Many, many people fall into this category. The kind of insole I have in mind is something like a "Conformable" and they are available at good outdoor shops and will take about half an hour to mould and fit. Make sure you have your boots with you. Also ensure that you have the right kind of insole - one that flexes (or doesn't) with your boot. They are also available for running shoes.

Once again be wary of believing everything that the manufacturers tell you, or you'll be disappointed when your boots don't make you tea in the morning and you find that you are tired at night...

Basically, there are three types of boot available: lightweight, medium weight and winter/heavy weight. A few words about boots before you decide what's for you

Whilst modern boots are worlds away from the predecessors of even ten years ago, they still need some breaking in. Wearing a boot in a shop for one hour is only going to indicate major faults, and you are going to have to move around in your new boots for four or five hours to find out if they have any other more subtle faults. So, your first day in new boots should be inside. If they don't fit most shops will either refund your money or exchange newly purchased boots provided they are still out-of-the-box squeaky clean. So don't get them dirty until you're sure that they are the ones for you.

Watch out for movement of the heel, which will cause blisters, and pressure points which in turn will cause numbness and possible nerve damage.

Chart on types of boot and their use

Type	Ideal activity	Do you have weak ankles?	Are you heavy for your size?	Heavy sack?	Wet Conditions?	Scree?	Snow?	Crampons?	Cold (below 0°C)
LIGHT	Day Walks	✗	✗	✗	✗	✗	?	?	✗
MEDIUM	Hill-walking Rough paths	✓	✓	✓	✓	✓	✓	?	?
HEAVY	Above snowline Very rough Wet conditions Mountaineering	✓	✓	✓	✓	✓	✓	✓	✓

Tightness will cause cold feet, and forward movement will give you sore or bruised toes when descending. If you are prone to Achilles tendon problems then ensure your ankles are held firmly at the sides, preventing the tendon from being rubbed.

Seams leak, just as sure as ducks swim. The more seams the bigger the pond. Leather leaks, but is easier to waterproof than fabric. All rubber soles slip on wet rock, cheap rubber soles slip on just about everything. It is generally assumed that the rougher the conditions, the stiffer the boot required. This is achieved by means of a $^3/_4$ internal shank (stiff) or a full internal shank (rigid). A boot with a rubber rand is going to last longer and hopefully protect your toes. A well fitting boot, regardless of its purpose, should first feel comfortable, allowing movement of the toes, without any at the heel. The amount of support required depends on the combined weight of you and your load going through your ankles. This may necessitate you going for a heavier boot than shown in the chart.

A good cobbler will be able to stretch out leather to give the odd carbuncle a bit more room, and plastic boots can be "blown" to alleviate tight spots. Usually reserved for ski-boots, this technique involves heating the plastic outer shell and then pushing out the side using a small hydraulic jack. As the shells of climbing boots are thinner plastic than ski boots extreme caution must be taken, and the operator must be an expert. Inner boots can also be altered with a hand grinder if they are too tight, or packed out with foam wedges to create a tighter fit. All these processes are irreversible so consider your plight and course of action carefully before handling your boots over for customising....

Some things never change, and a sock is still a sock. Correct? Not now. Whilst still called socks they've changed too, also for the better. Wool has always been the traditional material, and whilst technology has leapt forward in kangaroo bounds, it's pleasant to see that wool hasn't been replaced entirely, but has been mixed with newer materials to create a harder wearing, warmer, new generation alternative. Wool/acrylic/nylon mixes are the common choice now, with nylon being the second, cheaper choice. Construction methods too have progressed considerably. Whilst wool is still knitted, the density and thickness of the stitches can vary enormously within a sock to create reinforcement where it's needed most, at the toes and heel, and also to create padding for the soles and shins. Clever stuff. Nylon has been whipped into a frenzy with "loop stitch" construction in differing thicknesses to suit various conditions and warmth requirements.

For light and medium use boots, one pair of socks is usually enough, but many people do like to wear a thin cotton or wool sock under their big woolly ones, especially with plastic boots. Wool socks will wick away sweat under normal circumstances and will definitely stay warm but cotton, whilst comfortable, are really bad news inside walking boots. As are "sport" socks. They are not designed for this kind of use, as they can wear through rapidly

Hot desert, Jebel Sahro, Morocco

and unevenly, creating all sorts of problems. Even the good ones.

A change of footwear at the end of the day is bliss, a pair of training shoes or sandals being the common choice. Trainers are probably more versatile and, nowadays, very light, but there are some excellent sandals available which are easily adjusted to allow socks to be worn with them, and which have cleated soles to stop you sliding about. Whichever you choose take some light socks along too, just to give your toes a treat at the end of the day.

EYES

Eye protection is crucial on trek, particularly above the snowline and at altitude. Being high up, whether in the snow or not, leaves you open to more ultraviolet light because of the rarified atmosphere. Snow blindness is painful beyond description and to all intents and purposes disabling. It can also have a long lasting effect, so avoid it at all costs.

The only dependable protection is 100% UV block sunglasses and they don't come cheap. But you can't buy new eyes so spend, spend, spend. "Glacier" specs have side flaps which stop the sun sneaking in at the sides. They are also pretty good at stopping dust and snow, and a good alternative to goggles.

Glacier specs are available, to order, with prescriptive lenses. They are expensive due to the hand formed, pear shaped lenses most specs have. A few

Cold desert, the Hongu Valley, Nepal

pairs ("Julbo" to name one) have round lenses and your local optician will be able to order you round, shaped, 100% UV filter lenses to your prescription for about half the cost. If you are going to be in Asia for a while, have a pair made there for about a tenth of the cost in the UK.

Goggles can be made with prescription lenses but they cost about the same as a family car and are really made for professional skiers rather than occasional trekkers. Several manufacturers - Smith, Carrera and others - make goggles with a blown lens to allow spectacles to be worn underneath, a far more sensible alternative.

Whether goggles are carried is up to the individual. As I said, I find I can cope in all situations with my well-fitting glacier specs, but I would never fault anyone for carrying both, particularly above the snowline, where UV is reflected off the snow to dazzle you from underneath.

Mountain Guides will not take anyone across a glacier or snowfield without wearing eye protection. No argument. Protect your eyes.

SLEEPING BAGS AND MATS
All sleeping bags work on the same principle. They trap the warmth that our bodies generate and radiate. This stops us from getting cold, and saves our energy. Various materials trap it in various ways to various degrees of success. All sleeping bags are given the same overall grades: 1-5 seasons.

ONE SEASON - These bags are usually for taking to parties and crashing on people's floors or sleeping in well insulated caravans.

TWO SEASON - Definitely a summer sleeping bag, preferably in the south of France. Also ideal for boat, home and caravan.

THREE SEASON - At last, a useful sleeping bag. Suitable for most temperature and hot desert treks and the odd night above the snowline. Good for camping in the UK apart from the dead of Scottish winter.

FOUR SEASON - As the grade implies, good for use throughout the year, although who in their right minds camps in the winter? Covers trek up to and including the Alpine Region, in and about the snowline.

FIVE SEASON - Five seasons? This is just a hyper-warm rating that covers every imaginable cold situation, ie. cold deserts, high altitude and Norwegian films. The ideal bag for those who enjoy losing weight at night.

The two main fillings are down - from either duck or goose, or for lower rated bags, a feather and down mixture - and man-made fibres such as Holofil or Quadrofil. Down is light and can be compacted into very small spaces indeed but is hopeless when it's wet. Holofil and its contemporaries on the other hand are bulky, heavier, but warm when wet.

To stop the filling ending up at the bottom of your sleeping bag, keeping only your toes warm, it's kept in a series of compartments sewn together with a clever overlap to prevent cold spots (called "baffling"). This is an important feature as it makes the sleeping bag more efficient, but is harder to manufacture, so costs more. This is the reason that many down sleeping bags are given two ratings - the first describes the amount, in grammes, of down contained in the bag, the second describes the efficiency of the sleeping bag, known as the "fill power". It is possible therefore to have two sleeping bags with the same amount of filling, but for one to be 25% more efficient. They won't cost the same because the efficient bag will have a complicated baffle system, which is time-consuming to manufacture. The cost in time is passed on to us, the consumer. Having a warm, comfortable sleeping bag is the trekking equivalent to hot chocolate and a log fire on a winter evening at home. They allow a perfect finish to any kind of day, the chance to give your batteries an overnight charge and, perhaps, wake up with a smile. Bad ones give you eight hours of hell. As an informed individual, make your choice!!

Other features worth considering are: a zip for ventilation and heat control (and being sociable), a neck cuff that acts like a scarf, and a hood.

If you have a down bag you'll also want a liner. This keeps your bag clean and protects it from the damaging oils we exude during the night. If you don't use a liner then use your thermals as pyjamas. All sleeping bags seem to suffer when washed, and if it's not done properly they can be ruined, even with artificial fillings. Do not attempt to dry clean your sleeping bag or it will fall to pieces very shortly afterwards. Down bags must be washed with a special liquid soap available from good outdoor shops. Follow the instructions carefully and pay particular attention to drying the bag. It's almost inevitable that some of the feathers will be broken up and that you'll lose a bit of loft.

The man-made fillings are easily washed in a washing machine but again care must be exercised when drying - too hot and you'll end up with a Lilliputian version of the bag you put in. (Ask my dog why she happens to lie on an old sleeping bag.) It's just a case of heat and nylon not mixing, and 90% of all sleeping bags have a fair amount of nylon in them.

Back to liners. A good liner can add a season to your sleeping bag as well as protect it. They can be made from fibre pile, cotton or polypropylene. For a little extra warmth and a whole load of luxury try one made from silk. Expensive here, cheap in Asia, and held in high regard by those who spend lots of time at altitude.

Avoid rolling up your sleeping bag in a set method as this creates, over a period, seams which create cold spots. This applies to all kinds. Instead they should be crammed into a stuff-sack in a random manner. Voluminous synthetic bags can be compacted to a more manageable size with a compression sack (feathers become broken in this process) - simply a stuff-sack with a basic tape and buckle system that acts as a lever, reducing the sleeping bag to its smallest possible size. Try and allow your bag to be out and open as much as you can to give the filling room to expand and avoid damage, preferably inside out which allows the fresh air into the bag and denies fleas and bed bugs any warmth or hiding places. Storage at home or when not in use should be loose - in your airing cupboard or hanging up in the wardrobe. Extra large netting bags are available especially for this and are a worthy purchase.

A bivi bag can be a handy bit of kit on trek, allowing a comfortable night beneath the stars, or a dry night in a damp tent. The latter often happens during the winter or at altitude where condensation freezes inside the tent during the coldest part of the night, only to thaw with first light or the stove being lit. They range in design from simple envelopes to almost small tents complete with mosquito netting and hoops to give a bit of clearance for the head. The principal considerations are: the size (they should be roomy enough for you, your boots and a day sack; the number of seams (seams leak, remember); and the material (any fabric as long as it is breathable).

"A good blanket in lightweight cashmere or other woollen material, in a warm colour is a refinement which will not only give the tent a warm cosy appearance but, of more importance, will counteract the chilliness that is going to strike up through the uncovered ground sheet; particularly after sun-down." So advised A.L. Pullen in the *Cycling Handbook* of 1950. Mr Pullen didn't mention the lumps and bumps that strike up through the groundsheet after sun down, probably, I suspect because in 1950 there was no real portable solution. Thankfully now there are many, mostly due to spin-offs from the oil industry and the good old Space Programme. Lightweight, high density foam is the stuff, first utilised by the British firm Karrimor in their famous Karrimats, a name that has come to represent all sleeping mats. These simple mats are relatively cheap, robust, hard wearing, light and compact but most importantly are very effective at keeping out the chills and levelling out the ground, the two jobs they're purchased to do. Variations on the close-cell mat are around. Some are a sandwich of different densities to increase their principal properties and effectiveness whilst others have adopted a new approach and offer the mattress-equivalent of the string vest, where a warm air is trapped in pockets beneath the sleeper.

For most situations a simple mat will suffice and for the few extra pence and grammes it will cost, one that stretches from head to toe rather than head to hip. Prior to the development of closed cell foam mats, airbeds were a popular, but heavy alternative to sleeping on a pile of spare clothes, and recently a foam/airbed hybrid has been developed that supersedes both - the self-inflating sleeping mat, the Therm-a-Rest. Not much heavier than a foam mat, a Therm-a-Rest is the next best thing to a quality, fully sprung mattress. Its lightness will extend to your wallet too. But what price is too high for a good night's sleep? Buy one. And buy a puncture repair kit for it at the same time - but take heart, they don't need to be inflated to be effective.

TENTS

Although there are single skin tents on the market, they have a tendency to be expensive because they are made from breathable fabric. They also have a tendency to be poor performers because under normal conditions it's very hard to achieve the temperature difference required to allow breathing to occur! See the paragraph on jackets. During cooking the difference is too great for the fabric to cope. In both cases condensation runs down the roof of the tent. Uncomfortable at best, dangerous at worst, as this can freeze, severely inhibiting outflow.

Double skin tents surmount these problems by having an inner and outer skin. The inner, made from what is often little more than mosquito netting and a ground-sheet, allows vapour through to condense on the outer or fly, where it either drains off onto the ground or is absorbed by the atmosphere. The gap between fly and inner allows a healthy air-flow because the ground-sheet is sewn onto the inner only. Very cold conditions will see some condensation drip onto and freeze on the inner and most mountain tents will have a "pig's snout" ventilator to try and prevent this.

Some of the tents on the market are art-forms, utilising the most modern materials in the most imaginative ways to create tents of amazing strength and versatility. Geodesic domes with steep, space saving walls and carbon fibre poles now offer more cubic metres of luxury than is really deserved. But these are complicated beasts, so make sure that you are well practised at pitching your tent, especially in the wind, and have an appropriate repair kit, especially for poles. Add some shock cord to the list, to extend the peg-down points on

Climbing Mera, Nepal's highest and most popular trekking peak *(Author)*

Lobuche Peak East, Nepal - more technically demanding than Mera. Lobuche West is harder still and demands an expedition permit. In the background is Nuptse and Everest, with the Western Cwm in between *(Author)*

Inoffensive photography - Jebel Sahro tribeswomen, Morocco *(Author)*

Local occupations often make interesting pictures - planting rice in
Yunnan province, China *(W. Unsworth)*

nylon fly-sheets as the fly-sheets have a tendency to shrink when exposed to high doses of UV. You may even be forced to trim down your tent poles. The process isn't reversed by a two-week camping holiday in rainy Fort William. (If it can do that to a tent what do these rays do to our skin?)

For most trekking situations the following maxims apply.

1. Can this tent be erected fly-sheet first by someone without a doctorate in engineering? It's common sense to place the bit that's going to be wet up first...in case it's wet when you're putting it up.
2. Is the tent big enough? You want to have room to get all your kit and yourself inside otherwise the bits left outside may take it on themselves to go for a walk or get soaked. Is there enough room to cook under the fly-sheet? Tropical storms, snow showers and plagues of locusts have a tendency to arrive at suppertime.
3. Can I carry this tent? Or can your porters...can the airlines? Weight is always a trade-off against strength and size, but it has to be considered if it has to be carried.

RUCKSACKS AND HOLDALLS

Why have I mentioned holdalls here? Well if you are going to have most of your baggage carried by a beast of burden, whether human or otherwise, then a rucksack, with all its straps, flaps and pockets, is not ideal. During a trek, it is very unlikely that your luggage will be carried by itself: more likely it will be tied up with another of its ilk (or two, or more) to make a load. Protuberances will catch, snag and tear, regardless of their method of carriage. The other problem is that when a rucksack is carried by porters, the straps will be utilised to carry the whole load, ie. the weight of your rucksack with two others and a tent strapped to it, until they break.

Porters are not the only people who tend to be a bit rough with your baggage - airport baggage handlers are masters at rough trade. So again, the fewer pockets there are to rip off, the fewer buckles there are to break, the fewer straps to pull out and the fewer zips to completely mangle, the better the odds of your baggage arriving in usable condition. At least two manufacturers are making trekking bags, although one is completely off the mark by having zip pockets in the sides. Ex-army kit bags are very robust, reasonably priced, lockable and hold just about the right amount of gear. The down side is that they are awkward to carry and very hard to rummage about in. Retrieving something stashed at the bottom involves completely unpacking the beast. Trekking bags or holdalls, with their length-long zips, facilitate ease of entry, at the expense of introducing a major weakness in the bag, ie. the zip. So make sure any bag you use has a good strong zip. If the teeth in the zip are fine enough for that zip to be used in a piece of clothing, then they are too fine to be used in a trek bag. The zip pull should also have a hole in it, large enough to accommodate a small padlock. There should be a ring of some description on the end of the bag to allow it to be locked to something! No soft luggage is secure, but locking a zip will slow down or deter the opportunist thief.

Handles should be made of strong tape or webbing, and extend underneath the bag to increase the area of attachment, making it less likely to rip off and leave a hole at its anchor point.

Tie the handles of your kit bag together when it is to be handled by someone other than yourself - this prevents it being carried or dragged by one handle and reduces the risk of the zip opening or the handle being ripped off.

Commercial operators love trek bags, and most will either give you one when you've paid up, or sell you one cheap. In fact they were invented by them as a means of ensuring equality amongst clients (everyone carrying the same amount), and as an informal weight restrictor - how much can one put in a kit bag? It also simplifies porterage and they act as a mobile billboard. The reason most tour operators want you to limit your weight is, of course, economics as they employ less porters/hire less mules and because you are below your airline weight restriction the company can slip in some extras for the trek alongside the groups' luggage. Don't grumble because the alternatives are either more expensive trips or no extras. Extras cover things like Christmas puddings, chocolate, proper tea and toilet rolls (rationed).

If you are travelling with an organised party, all with identical bags, customise yours with some coloured tape or ribbon to make it easily identifiable. And don't forget some polythene bin bags to act as waterproof liners.

Daysacks

So you've packed your sleeping bag, air mattress, spare clothes, cuddly toy et al safely in your Kevlar reinforced, fall-out proof kit bag, and waved it goodbye until the evening. But still lying around are all the bits and pieces you need to see you through the day - extra clothes, waterproofs, sun-block, cameras, shades, the complete works of Shakespeare, and of course your water bottles - for which you need a daysack.

As your daysack contains your daytime life support system, it is very important that you get a good one. A poorly constructed daysack will die on trek, but not before it's dragged its wearer through agony by being so uncomfortable, and shed its contents all over the trail through perforated seams, fragile buckles and ripped cloth. So buy a sack that's tough.

Before you think about what shape or size the daysack should be, think about your own shape and size. Even a quality sack is going to be uncomfortable if it doesn't fit properly. A well fitting sack will have a padded waistbelt keeping the weight on your hips, with the padded shoulder straps coming off the sack just below the nape of the neck, and spaced wide enough apart so as not to pinch that tender neck. The waistbelt must be easily adjusted to allow for one's ever changing waistline. (This has rather more to do with adding and removing clothing than anything to do with food intake.) This can be a

A strong simple kit bag is best

problem for people of a slight build as those with little waists often find that waistbelts are too big, or rather will not cinch up sufficiently, preventing them from getting the weight of the sack correctly distributed onto the hips. This leaves the shoulders to bear an excessive proportion of the weight, and the back to suffer under the strain.

As mentioned, shoulder straps should be wide and padded, and not too close together at the point where they leave the sack. Again, slightly built people may have a problem here, with the shoulder straps being too wide apart at the top, making the sack uncomfortable. The only solution is to buy one that fits you. Many suppliers nowadays offer specially proportioned equipment for smaller people and women's frames. Many daysacks these days can have a chest-strap running between the shoulder straps. Most don't actually supply this as standard but offer it as an optional feature. I recommend them as I think they help create a more stable load, but for me an additional important function is to temporarily allow the shoulder straps to be loosened, letting the pack weight fall to the hips and creating a cooling airspace up your back. Chest straps also offer an ideal vehicle for carrying cameras and binoculars - see 'Photography'.

I haven't seen a daysack with a full frame for a long time, but they do exist, and like pitbull terriers, are best handled by someone else. Some have small, basic internal frames, usually two flat metal strips, but my own experience is that they either escape out of the sack at the bottom, as they create a hard spot more susceptible to abrasion, or they get completely mangled when being loaded onto planes, boats, trains, mules or hotel bellboys. Frameless bags are also easier to cram into overhead lockers or under the seats in aeroplanes.

This brings us to volume. For day to day trekking, and aeroplane journeys, a 35 to 40 litre rucksack is about ideal. There is a good choice of bags in this range because trekkers, climbers, mountaineers and even skiers find this such a convenient size. Trekkers tend to need lots of little things easily to hand such as sunblock, knives, gloves, toilet paper etc. Zipped pockets are the ideal place for them, but be wary when buying a daysack with side pockets that protrude to the point of being a hindrance. You probably don't realise how far back you swing your arms until you've carried a sack with large pockets.... Don't be shy about marching up and down the floor of your local outfitters when trying out a new rucksack.

Climbing and mountaineering sacks don't usually have side pockets because in climbing situations they not only restrict movement but also catch on things when you definitely don't want anything to catch. Many have side tension straps which tighten up the load, keeping it nice and snug to the back. The same straps can be used to carry small pockets, ski poles, jackets or anything else you like to the side of the sack.

Like kit bags, no one has managed to make a completely waterproof and dustproof rucksack, so you'll need a liner to go inside it. Bin liners will do at a push or if you have agricultural connections, a fertiliser bag. If you have no connections but lots of money you can buy a custom made bag in polythene or nylon. Whatever, make sure you have one. Your local supermarket will supply small waterproof bags for all your other bits and pieces - spare clothes, first-aid kit, etc.

Some of the more whacky designs on the go just now utilise a lot of zips, and whilst some of them are excellent I would be wary of taking them on trek - a broken buckle can be substituted with a piece of cord, but how do you close your sack if the zip has broken? It can be rough out there in Trekland and even the toughest can succumb to the rigours, so carry a small repair kit just in case: a darning needle, dental floss (as good as mariner's waxed cotton), a spare buckle or two, a patch of canvas or heavy duty nylon, and some bits of cord.

Large stuff-sacks keep the contents of your kit bag or rucksack organised and save time and clutter when you are packing and unpacking. It's easy and quick to throw six or eight stuff-sacks in and out of your kit bag; they stop your clean clothes from mingling with your laundry and prevent your spare batteries from hiding in your spare socks. Despite the name, they shouldn't be stuffed (sleeping bags and duvet exempt) because if they are loose and floppy

Sub-Alpine,
Monte Rotondo,
Corsica

then they will nestle down together and save space. Because they aren't under stress and don't need to be waterproof (remember, your bag has a polythene layer...) then they can be made at home from any light, available material. Different colours avoid confusion, and on light coloured materials the bag's contents can be written on the outside with marker pen. Now, that is being smart and organised. A stuffsack about half the size of a pillow case is about ideal.

STOVES AND FUELS
In Europe, the United States, Australia and New Zealand a multitude of stoves are available plus the fuels to fire them. Further from home the availability of fuel is going to decide your choice of trekking stove and hopefully that of your service crew too. Wood fires are definitely out on ecological grounds and, where possible, try to persuade your porters/agent/trekking company likewise. Let's have a look at what fuels are available and see how they fit in with the trekking scene.

Butane and Propane
Clean and easy to use and readily available in Europe and the States, cooking by propane used to be done whilst watching paint dry, but the latest generation

of propane or butane stoves is right up there with the best, fast burning and a good choice if the fuel is readily available. For group cooking, the bottles are heavy and unwieldy - no problem for a mule though. For one or two people the canisters and stoves are light and convenient, and are becoming popular in North Africa and South America. Sadly, propane or butane cannot be exported by aeroplane and shipping it, whilst possible, is not economical or practical for a one-off trek or even a small expedition. If using propane up high, then allow one small canister per pair per day.

Petrol (Auto Gas, White Gas)
Petrol is quite a good fuel, and readily available out of the petrol pump throughout the world. Automotive petrol has many additives which make it burn well in an internal combustion engine but can damage camping stoves, and even those designed to take petrol need careful maintenance to ensure efficient burning, the main problem being that it gums up the main jet and fuel lines which necessitates frequent cleaning.

White Gas (Coleman Fuel) eliminates these problems, but once again cannot be transported by plane. All petrol has the potential to flare up, and create carbon monoxide as a by-product, so no cooking inside the tent, I'm afraid. Its availability does make it very attractive though. White Gas is quite popular in South America.

Paraffin (Kerosene)
Almost as common throughout the world as petrol, used particularly in Asia, paraffin is less clean than its more refined relations whilst burning or during storage. Burned under pressure, paraffin needs a more volatile spirit (meths, petrol, alcohol paste or "meta" bars) to prime the stove until it creates its own heat to vaporise the paraffin. This reluctance to vaporise makes paraffin a nightmare if split, as its soot, its smell and greasy feel permeate and linger, making it very hard to dispose of in primitive washing conditions. Outside the first world, paraffin is prone to be diluted either with water or diesel, reducing its efficiency and clogging up the jets and fuel lines of your stoves. Grit, dead flies and nail clippings are not uncommon accidental paraffin additives, so be prepared to filter it prior to filling your stove. An old stocking folded over several times will do in an emergency. Allow 10-15 litres per day for a group of 10 to 15 trekkers plus attendant crew for trek if you don't want to resort to burning wood. Which you don't.

Stoves for small groups
Out of the four fuels mentioned, petrol and paraffin have the most in common, being burned under pressure in similar types of stove. So similar in fact that for several years now MSR have made a stove that will burn either fuel by simply switching over the burner jet. Other manufacturers have taken their

Comfort is where it's at ... typical trekking lunch

lead, and there is a good choice of multi-fuel stoves on the market now. If you don't know what fuels will be available in Trekland then a multi-fuel stove should be a serious consideration.

Stoves for large groups
Large groups need big stoves. Stoves that cost a lot to freight and purchase, and a bit of a waste if you get to Trekland only to find they are unsuitable. It's easier and simpler to buy out there and often a lot, lot cheaper too. Throughout South America and Asia there are locally made stoves for locally available fuels. Designed (sometimes...) for domestic use they are easily adapted for trekking.

Carrying and storage
Fuels should not be stored or carried in plastic containers but, in practice, metal jerry cans are either too heavy or unavailable, leaving plastic cans or nothing. For small parties or short trips, where there is no need to take a large amount of fuel, then lightweight alloy bottles are available but they are not cheap. Polythene bottles are, but I didn't say to use them.... Empty fuel containers are as dangerous as full ones when it comes to taking them on the plane, or leaving them lying around in the sun; the fumes are most volatile.

Either remove the tops, to allow the fumes to escape, or refill the container with water.

If you are taking your own stove out from the UK then make sure you have a spares kit with you (jet, washers, prickers, filters, etc.) and if you have had your stove serviced prior to going out test it to make sure that it has been serviced properly. 20,000ft up in the Himalaya is no place to find out that your stove is set up to burn petrol when you've lugged along 40 litres of paraffin. Correct, Peter? Yes, it happened, and I promised I wouldn't mention it.... I've seen a bit of hair out of a horse's tail used as a pricker, but best take a few packets out on trek with you - just in case there aren't any horses around.

CAMERAS AND PHOTOGRAPHY

The number of serious photographers now coming on trek has warranted this seemingly over-the-top chapter on cameras. Trekking and photography do make good bedfellows provided the camera is treated properly, and that discretion and thought are used when photographing your fellow human beings.

No matter how good a photograph is, it is no substitute for having been there and seen it. No one I know has a photo collection that can compare with the images that I have in the Great Photo Album of my Mind. Eat your heart out Galen Rowell. And no matter how much money has been spent on photographic equipment, the most important piece is the bit that is three inches behind the viewfinder - you.

There are two kinds of photo - those that represent a picture diary of your trip, and those that are creative images. I'm not going to indulge in philosophical discussions, but let me say that I think you would be silly not to take a camera on trek because there will be moments that you will want to record visually, and compositions and colours that will cry out too loudly to be ignored.

Film - idiot's guide

If you've never considered yourself a photographer and only want a stack of photos to stick in your scrapbook and pass round the office, then go for print film. Cheap(ish) films are readily available, but for that once-in-a-lifetime trip, best pamper yourself and go for quality brands - Kodak or Fuji at around 100 ASA - and have them processed through a reputable camera shop. ASA or ISO is a measure of film speed. The difference in quality will show when you have enlargements made. When a print is blown up you'll notice the grain - all the little dots of colour that make up the photo - and the bigger the print the grainier it will become. To get round this, buy film with a lower ASA, say 64 or 50. The catch here is that the lower the ASA, the greater the amount of light needed to properly expose the film. One way of allowing more light into the camera is to open the shutter for a longer period of time, ie. a slow shutter speed. So far so good? But cameras need to be held very steady at slow shutter speeds, so you'll need to prop up the camera on either a bean bag or tripod.

Another, better way of producing quality enlargements is to use slide film (transparencies). Slide film, when projected, is able to reproduce a greater range of colours than print film. The colour range stands out and is apparently less grainy, despite having a comparable ASA. It is also possible to project the picture to sizes inconceivable with print film. Quality slide film is expensive, and they are not so convenient for showing around the office. Good prints can be made easily, but relatively expensively, from slides: slides from prints not so, I'm afraid.

It is best to buy film in the UK before flying out, as quality and stocks cannot be guaranteed in Trekland. There is considerable controversy over the effect of airport x-rays on film. Several independent testers have concluded that with film in the 25-200 ASA range it requires in the region of at least two dozen passes through a machine to have any effect. Personally, I don't trust the machines and insist wherever possible on a hand search. Sometimes I get it, others not, but so far have never lost a film. Some people swear by their "filmsafe" lead-lined bags, an x-ray proof bag, commonly available in camera shops. However when one of these passes through the x-ray machine and the operator cannot see into it, he or she simply cranks up the power to get a good look. Result? Possibly a larger x-ray dose than normal!

Care of films at home is easy - keep them in the fridge. On trek it is not so easy: the cold is not a problem but the heat and dust can be. Wrap them up in

Sometimes the land just shouts 'Photograph me!'

a polythene bag and bury them deep in the heart of your kit bag or rucksack where hopefully your luggage will act as insulation from the heat. Don't keep them in the top or outside pocket where a good frying is a distinct possibility. It is worth removing the film from the depths of your pack at night and allowing it to become cool.

Number your films and use them in sequence, and note the details of the first shot on each to give a clue as to where to start when you come home. ALWAYS completely rewind films, pulling the film leader back into the cassette: this should prevent you from double-exposing the film and ending up with Mount Everest emerging from the head of a yak! If you are really organised then the first photograph on each film will be of a piece of paper with the film number written on it. Extreme? Not if the postman delivers thirty boxes of slides to your house on the same day.... If you are really, really smart you'll note the details of all your shots on all your films.... A common mistake is not threading the film on properly to the take-up spool in the camera, resulting in the film not moving as you wind and snap that once-in-a-lifetime scene. How do you know if you've done it properly? Very simple! If your camera is a mechanical one, with a wind-on lever, you will have a rewind lever on the opposite side. If your film is winding on correctly the rewind lever will move anti-clockwise. Electronic cameras have a small electronic signal on their display to warn you - read the instruction book before you go!!

Cameras

The three main camera killers on trek are dust, the cold and damp. Good accessories can help reduce the chances of damage or death, but life expectancy will be given a boost if you have a tough camera to start off with. So have a quick look through the camera magazine and talk to the camera shop staff to find out what's around and recommended, and what can be afforded. New isn't necessarily best, despite what the ads say. Most of the photos in this book were taken with a 15-year-old, very basic camera.

The big decision will be whether to go for an SLR (Single Lens Reflex) or a compact camera - the latter small and light, usually with built-in flash and automatic focusing and exposure. One that uses standard 35mm film and possibly with a zoom facility as well. The other option, the SLR is characterised by the viewfinder image being that of the view through the lens. What you see is what you photo. Traditionally SLRs allowed a flexibility, through their interchangeable lenses and filters, denied to compact cameras. This still may be the case but the gap is a lot narrower than it used to be with the better compacts outperforming poorer SLRs. Many people carry both - with print film in their compact and slides in the SLR. Some carry three and even four cameras with accessories, an extreme situation where, I feel, the photograph has taken over from the privilege of being and seeing.

Camera cases

Regardless of whether you go compact or SLR the first consideration is looking after your camera on trek, and the first step towards camera care is to buy a quality case for it. There are several padded camera cases on the market just now with all the right qualifications - robust materials and construction, well fitting so the camera doesn't move around inside, with ease of access and good protection from abrasive dust and the elements. Some have accessory pockets for filters and lenses but they don't come cheap. Don't be tempted to buy a cheap look-a-like at half the price - it won't seem such a bargain when a buckle breaks or the stitching comes out and your camera sails off down the ridge, or into the river.

Cleaning kit

Definitely next on the list - a simple puff-brush and a lens cloth is all you need.

Spares and other accessories

Two sets of spare batteries should be taken, especially if your camera has an electronic shutter and if you are going up high - batteries freeze in the cold, so make sure you have a spare set in your inside pocket where they'll be nice and warm.

A "sky light" filter for each lens protects the end element from dust, scratches and even the odd knock without affecting the camera's performance at all. It also helps eliminate colour casts and penetrate haze.

A tripod and/or a bean-bag is also a pretty handy gizmo to have around, especially when the light is low, but good tripods have a tendency to be heavy, and light ones tend to blow over or break. A bean bag is a good second choice - there is usually someone around with a tripod when nothing else will do. If you are trekking with friends then obviously arrange to have a communal one - and then fall out with each other at the first spectacular sunset...and of course, if appropriate, don't forget your shutter release cable.

SLR extras

If you are a photographer then you'll have a pretty good idea of what you'll want to take with you, and far from me to say what you should or shouldn't carry. However, too much camera gear can be a real encumbrance and like an unruly child can start to run your life. Having had clients on trek who had to hire their own porter to carry their camera gear, I was very apprehensive when I was asked to escort a professional photographer in Morocco for a week - Lisle Denis - but I was pleasantly surprised and inspired by how little gear she carried. In fact, it could almost fit into the pockets of her waistcoat. Here is a list of what she took, by way of inspiration to you, and show how little one really needs. I must add that all her equipment was of best quality, and all 35mm.

2 x camera bodies (Contax)
1 x tripod (howitzer strength)
1 x 20mm lens
1 x 35-70 zoom lens (with rubber lens hood)
1 x 70-210 zoom lens (with rubber lens hood)
1 x 2x converter

FILTERS -   Graduated Blue   Graduated Tobacco
Polariser
Dedicated flash gun
Spare batteries (lots of)
Cleaning kit/jeweller's screwdrivers
Film - 300 rolls if I remember rightly

Exposing for snow (and sand)
Snow can play nasty tricks with exposure meters, so if in doubt take a full sun exposure, then cut it back by one stop. Or use the "Sunny 16" rule. This dictates that you set your lens aperture to f16 and your shutter speed to the nearest equivalent shutter speed to your film ASA setting, eg. for 50 or 64 ASA film set 60th sec. or for 100 ASA set 125th sec. This will give a correct full sun exposure. As snow is white and a natural reflector you will need to reduce your setting by one f stop, ie. from 16 to 22. If in any doubt read the bit of paper with exposure info. on it that came with your film - it is very accurate.

Carrying your camera on trek
Without doubt the safest place to carry your camera is in your rucksack, however, it is not the most convenient place, and to make the most of photo opportunities the camera should be very close to hand. Compacts lend themselves to being very accessible - snuggling into a breast pocket, or in a case on your rucksack waist belt, or even on a strap round the neck. SLRs being heavier and bulkier are not so versatile and require more thought as to how they should be carried. Spare lenses, flashes etc. can easily be housed on waistbelt straps in padded cases. SLRs can be worn like side-arms, but this prevents you from putting your hands, or anything else, in your pockets and wears out trousers at the side.

I use a system whereby I wear my camera across my chest and utilise the rucksack so that it bears the weight. Place the camera round the neck. Clip the strap onto the haul loop (between shoulder straps) with a small carabiner. Pass the rucksack chest strap through loops on the camera bag. Clip the camera bag to left, or right rucksack strap.

Lens caps
Carry a spare! These can be attached via leashes to the camera, a worthwhile

A realistic photo of an Asian child - the price? Helping rack sheaves for half an hour

accessory. If leashes seem expensive, or in an emergency, make your own with some fine cord, elastic bands and some super-glue.

Photographic no-no's
Military or police personnel or installations
Airports or military aircraft
Women - Islamic/Hindu countries in particular

ASK FIRST if it's OK to photo
Place of worship
Religious festivals and occasions (funerals, weddings)
In museums and other public buildings
Dodgy profession - drugdealer, gangsters, prostitutes, etc
Portraits - ask first or be very, very discreet, ie. long lens and good cover
If in doubt simply smile, show your camera and gauge the reaction.

BITS AND PIECES
These are a few odds and ends to fill your rucksack and make life on trek a little more comfortable:
SAK: (Swiss Army Knife) This needs no introduction or real explanation - just

make sure you have one on trek with you. There are some very neat and practical pouches/sheaths on the market to take any size of knife - buy one if you need to know exactly where you knife is at all times.

"WET WIPES": Until recently these were only available in small buckets with poorly fitting lids - not very practical on trek. Now they can be purchased in heavy polythene resealable packets and are very practical on trek. Antiseptic wipes are now available from chemists and, though their intended function is the cleaning of wounds, they are ideal for ensuring hands are germ-free before eating where the washing facilities are dodgy.

A MUG AND SPOON: Your own mug and spoon can have a very civilising effect on your day and increase your protection against cross-infection and poor hygiene when used in local cafes and houses...as long as they don't wash them for you. Stainless, plastic, ceramic - the choice is yours. Spoil yourself and go for an insulated polythene mug with a large handle and a lid with a spout and you'll know what luxury is at high camp, and reduce the risk of an in-tent spill. A spoon is essential in China to stave off malnutrition.

WHISTLE: To attract attention. A plastic one without a pea - moving parts freeze up high. Tie it to something, a zip pull or whatever, so that you don't lose it.

MIRROR: A small stainless steel mirror will help attract attention too. Also useful for looking at yourself (nasty) and holding over the mouths of unconscious people to check doubtful breathing. Even nastier.

NOTEBOOK AND PENCILS: Pens tend to leak and they cannot be sharpened with a SAK.

"ZIP LOCK" POLYTHENE BAGS: Useful for lots of reasons from acting as map cases to keeping your book dry, or as an emergency hat. Half a dozen will do.

ZINC OXIDE TAPE: Tapes things back together again, eg. pencils, tent poles and even fingers.

DENTAL FLOSS AND DARNING NEEDLE: As waxed cotton, and very strong, dental floss can be used to sew tears in rucksacks, kit bags, tents, etc. It costs a lot less than sailmaker's cotton, and comes in a conveniently sized pack. And of course it can also be used to clean teeth. Back up with a few scraps of heavy nylon to use as patches.

CIGARETTE LIGHTER: For post Andrex moments.

SOAP AND FLANNEL: For post cigarette lighter moments.

TOWEL: Bar towels are light, absorbent and very portable. Pertex towels tend to become waterlogged too easily and feel slimey. Take your choice.

HEAD TORCH: Head torches are like Swiss Army Knives - once you've become used to one it's hard to imagine how you managed without. The good ones are expensive but should be viewed as an unavoidable expense as the cheap ones are not up to the job. You'll need a spare battery, or three if it's going to be cold, plus a couple of spare bulbs. Halogen bulbs are easily found now

Discreet photography - no offence caused
Dapper shepherd, Otter Pradesh, India. Photo in exchange for examining
sore eye. Fair exchange!

Sub-Alpine, Pic du Midi, Central Pyrenees

and produce an amazing amount of light but soak up battery power and, in the majority of situations, a standard bulb will suffice. Head torches may look silly, but they are so practical: the light is always where you need it, ie. where you are looking, and your hands are free to do what you want them to do. Ever tried holding a torch in your teeth whilst you go to the loo?

Don't forget, batteries should always be carried in your hold luggage and take the battery out of your torch when flying to avoid it accidentally switching itself on.

TREKKING POLES: Trekking poles are a very sensible idea and they have recently become very popular. On descents they take some of the load from your knees and ankles and on ascents they enable you to involve your upper body muscles in the action. They should be collapsible, preferably in three pieces, so that they can be carried in your rucksack or kit bag when travelling. They can also be improvised for adjustable splints, stretcher poles and cattle prods. Experts use 2 poles, but one is better than nothing....

Clothing list
Temperate trek:
    Boots
    Trainers/sandals
    Heavy socks 2 pairs

    Underwear
    Thermal layer
    Shirt(s)

Light socks 2 pairs
Bandana
Sun hat
Balaclava
Gloves
Neckerchief

Waterproof jacket
Waterproof trousers

Pile jacket / sweater
Pile trousers
Light trousers / skirt
Shorts
T-shirts x 2

Gaiters

For above the snowline, or in extreme cold add:
Rigid leather or plastic boots
Thermal inner gloves
Heavy mits or gloves

Overmits
Duvet jacket

For hot desert trips bear in mind that it can become very cold very quickly - clothes should be as 'Temperate' trek.

Bits and pieces list (for rucksack)
Spare laces
Darning needle
Dental floss
Cloth scraps
Roll of tape
Swiss army knife

Wet wipes
Loo roll
Cigarette lighter
Mug and spoon
First-aid kit
Vaseline
Sunblock

Lip salve
Total block
Diary / notebook
Pens and pencils
Whistle
Mini wash kit
Book
Water bottles
Iodine
Sunglasses
Head torch
Trekking poles

and the rest...
Rucksack and liner
Kit bag and liners
Sleeping bag and liner
Toilet bag and towel
Boot maintenance kit (if appropriate)
Sleeping mat (and puncture kit if
    appropriate)

First-aid spares
Spare batteries
Padlock
Stuff bags
Crampons
Ice axe
Climbing gear (as required)

CHAPTER SEVEN
On trek

TREK ORGANISATION

A typical trekking day

This is a rough guide. Add or subtract an hour (or more) to the day's start depending on if you are on an easy or hard trek.

6.00	Wakey! Wakey! Usually a quiet start to the day with the kitchen boys bringing you a cup of tea in bed.
6.15	The kitchen boys bring a bowl of washing water. Wash.
6.30	Out of bed and packing.
6.45	Kit bag packed (very important - this allows porters to make up loads and get a head start).
6.50	Tent cleaned, collapsed and packed.
7.00	Breakfast.
7.30	Third pint of tea for the day
7.30-45	Start trekking.
8.15	Pass porters drinking tea at side of track.
9.30	Stop for tea and watch porters pass by.
12.30/13.00	Stop for lunch, read book, have snooze, wash some clothes.
14.30	Trekking starts again.
16.00/16.30	Arrive in camp, set up tent, wash, have tea and biscuits, write diary, etc.
18.00	Dinner and debrief, moans etc.
18.45	Briefing for following day.
20.00	Brush teeth, sort out rucksack for next day, go to sleep.

Typical Trek Leader's day

5.00	Head for cook tent and grab a brew.
5.30	Pack up kit and tent, have breakfast
5.35	Sort out lunch, makes sure there is enough water for everyone to fill bottles. Check enough loo paper and that loo hole is deep enough for morning rush.
6.15	Set up breakfast with cook-boys, check health (hold clinic), for service crew. Eat breakfast and drink tea.
6.30	Harass clients, help collapse and pack tents.
6.45	Check clients' health - hold clinic.
7.00	Harass clients into eating breakfast. Drink tea. Have second breakfast.
7.15	Harass clients to drink tea.

7.30	Harass clients into going trekking? Send guide with them - Sirdars' Assistant. Check campsite is clean, porters happy, nothing left behind - fill in toilet.
8.00	Walk until you start to meet group. Is the back member at the back because s/he wants to, or because s/he isn't feeling well?
9.45	Drink tea.
12.00/12.30	Catch up kitchen crew, check lunch site, prepare water for bottles - refill, sleep. Drink tea. Eat, sleep. Hold clinic.
14.30	Harass clients to start walking.
14.45	Check lunch site is clean, gather rubbish, start walking.
16.00	Arrive in camp, set up mess-tent, prepare water for kitchen/ mess tent. Dig loo hole, erect loo tent. Drink tea. Check all is OK with kitchen. Hold clinic.
18.45	Set out route for next day, arrange rendezvous, describe route, issue snacks, answer questions.
20.00	Check with kitchen about next day's food, give feedback on previous meal, drink tea and have chat with the boys.
21.00	Brush teeth, say prayers, go to bed.

Social Structures

Throughout the world the social structure on a trek is very much the same and the rules of behaviour ditto. It's a small monarchy with the Western Trek Leader (WTL) as king or queen. Next to them is real power, the chancellor, if you like, the Sirdar or local guide. Often the only difference twixt the Leader and the Sirdar is in fact that the Sirdar is employed by the agent, and the Leader employs the agent. It is a very tentative mark of rank. A strong willed Sirdar can make a Leader's life hell in much the same way as a Regimental Sergeant Major can destroy a young officer. The bottom line is that a trek Leader can sack a Sirdar. Not vice versa. And on trek, the buck stops at the Leader. The relationship between the Sirdar and his charges - the Service Crew - is quite straightforward. He is the boss, they are the workers. The relationship between the Leader and the client is not so easily defined. Whilst indirectly employed by his/her clients, the Leader has been empowered to make certain decisions on their behalf. The client pays to have decisions made for them, yet the leader has a professional obligation to keep his clients informed and offer choice wherever possible.

The relationship between the Sirdar and the WTL can vary enormously from one of almost two-way adoration to complete contempt. The key to a good relationship here is to have a Sirdar and Leader with mutual respect for each other, who are pulling together with one common aim - to give you, the client, the best holiday ever. A good Sirdar/Leader team will never be heard either shouting at each other, or anyone else. In fact, as good managers, they

Mera Peak, Nepal's highest and most popular trekking peak

will not appear to be doing very much at all. I'll talk about WTLs further on, not only from a client's point of view, but also from that of organising and leading your own trip.

The Sirdar will usually have a few deputies below him to help with the general running of things. One of these will be the cook. Sometimes the cook will have almost equal status with the Sirdar. Of course the cook has his helpers too, boys to prepare the vegetables and wash the dishes. The kitchen crew may even have a porter or two attached to them. Back to the Sirdar. Below his assistants are the porters. The guys who do most of the work. Or it could be horsemen or yak boys or muleteers. There is a very direct chain of command and it is very important to observe this and go through the proper channels. As a client, any complaint or request concerning the kitchen or porterage crew must be made via the WTL. He/she in turn will pass this on to the Sirdar or sometimes his assistants, who will then pass it down the line and vice versa.

This system ensures that everyone knows where they stand and stops clients pushing kitchen boys and porters around and, funnily enough, vice versa. It also saves a lot of time because Leaders and/or Sirdars are usually one step ahead and often have already spotted a weakness or discrepancy and have set wheels in motion to rectify the situation, prior to client/porter comment. It also means that the Sirdar/Leader can act as filters to block any unreasonable or possibly offensive, albeit innocent requests.

The real benefit of working this way is that because business goes through the Sirdar/Leader, the conversation and interaction between the client and service crew is of a purely social nature and this interaction has to be not only encouraged but is almost a reason for going trekking in itself. Who knows more about a country, its politics, its good points, its bad points, the colour of its soil, other than the man born and living there? What makes a tourist welcome? (other than his money!) Being friendly and interested in the host and his culture and not just his drink and beaches.

The Sirdar and Leader also act as quality control on each other, and a good partnership will happily give and accept constructive criticism. The clients and the service crew also have a line of complaint should they feel their respective leaders are out of line, ie. clients can go to the Sirdar, and service crew to the Leader, to be used with real discretion, however.

As a client or team member, it is very important to follow this procedure. On trips where there are two or more Leaders, one should always be appointed as overall in command. Even if you've organised your own trip and you're all mates, it's vital that the Sirdar has someone to report to, and take commands from. Otherwise confusion will arise, as anyone who has tried to work under two bosses can testify. On commercial trips without a WTL, beware of the potential inter-client power struggle that can happen, as described in section 2. So if the Sirdar looks after the service side of things, what does the WTL do apart from act as a figurehead? The bottom line is that his/her job is to bring everyone home safely, and as a bonus, give everyone a good holiday.

To safety, add health and you'll appreciate where most trek Leaders' worries are. Prevention being better than cure, it is the Leader's personal responsibility to ensure that the kitchen and clients have an adequate source of germ-free water and to see that hygiene levels are high and maintained. Should someone succumb to injury or illness it is then the Leader's job to treat that person, with knowledge and confidentiality, retaining the client's dignity. This responsibility also extends to the staff. So trek Leaders do have to know their first-aid and what's inside the drugs cupboard. I don't know how far their responsibility extends towards pack animals, but there are at least two WTLs out there who can shoe a mule....

Safety is a broad issue, but extends from issuing porters with sunglasses to rigging fixed ropes, to ensuring all clients are properly fed and equipped. The Leader, as the company's representative, is obliged to listen to people's complaints, act where it is possible and reasonable to do so, and log these complaints to report to the company as soon as possible. It's not the Leader's place to complain bitterly that it's not his/her fault and walk away.

It is the Leader's responsibility to try and install and maintain harmony within any group, to be aware of friction within the group and to smooth it out with minimum fuss.

Ensuring harmony may mean making decisions on behalf of the group when it is apparent that the group will not be able to come to an amiable agreement themselves - at least they'll only fall out with the Leader and not each other. The Leader is responsible for ensuring that clients are made aware of how they are expected to behave within a particular culture, and be firmly told if their behaviour is out of order.

Despite not being directly in charge of the service crews, the WTL is ultimately responsible for their health, safety and performance, interviewing the Sirdar if necessary. A common problem here is the penny-pinching of the Sirdar, either for himself or the Agent, by overloading and slowing down the porters. If you are leading make sure you have a spring balance with you. The Sirdar is also responsible for ensuring that all service crew are covered by insurance - check this, because if there is an accident, rest assured if there is no cover for those concerned it's the WTL who will be blamed. So check it out and give yourself some peace of mind.

WTLs have unavoidable responsibilities towards the service crew when going up high, onto the snowline, or onto glaciers. They must personally ensure that everyone has the proper equipment and clothing for the conditions, and have it checked before leaving to go on a trek. This may mean the WTL purchasing a stack of woolly hats, woolly jumpers and trousers, socks, boots, crampons and even ice-axes. If you wouldn't go on trek without any of these, why should your employees?

Of all things, a WTL must be patient and discrete. Every trek Leader has had a client on a trip they would rather not see again, but bad as they may have been, they still have the right of privacy. The WTL has no right to tell others, on consequent treks, about their anti-social behaviour, their illnesses or foolish acts, unless to make a point, but not for entertainment. Of course names should never be mentioned.

Constant reference to previous trekkers is not going to make your present group feel valued at all, and will only make them wary of talking to you, the WTL.

Good WTLs are as interested in people as the great outdoors and are generally better listeners than orators, better entertainers than mountaineers. A doctor friend of mine made the point that only prostitutes have clients. If this is so then WTLs are the prostitutes of the trekking world, and as such, must try their hardest to give customer satisfaction. So make sure if you are WTL that your clients feel cared for, and are kept informed of what's going on, and that you make it your personal business to know what's going on.

How to annoy your clients - advice to WTLs
1. Be late without offering an explanation.
2. Ask several times how much the clients have paid for their trip.
3. Tell the clients several times how many treks you have been on.

4. Tell the clients you don't pay for your equipment.
5. Start every sentence with "I had a really lovely client on the last trek".
6. Eat a fried egg sandwich whilst discussing a client's nausea/diarrhoea.
7. Snore at high camp.
8. Say "last week the weather here was beautiful" or "it's lovely to have a week of rain after three months of unending blue skies".
9. Ask them if they miss chocolate Hob Nobs/going down the pub/proper toilets.
10. Tell them they don't look well.
11. Tell them they aren't drinking enough tea/water.
12. Slurp your soup.

Sirdar's Assistants (SAs)

As deputies it is the assistants' job to do as the Sirdar dictates. These are the middle-management of the trekking world, the up and coming, learning the Sirdar's trade. Some, especially the young ones, let the power go to their heads a bit - as happens to us all on occasion....

The biggest problem with SAs is that they have a tendency to over-step the mark socially by either asking too many personal questions or just creeping into people's personal space. This can mainly be attributed to social immaturity and adolescent curiosity. There are often cases of SAs asking for "presents" and of them "borrowing" clients' possessions. Again, usually the younger ones. The older lads have usually learned the rules of Western society or have been thinned out. Usually, but not always, and some "wide boys" make it through to Sirdar, sad to say, considering the number of jobless good guys around.

Cooks and cook crew

These are the people who can make or break your trip, especially if the weather is bad and the visibility poor. At least if the food is good, then there is something going for slobbing around camp. There are three reasons why the food may be bad: the cook can't cook; the cook has only bad food to cook; the cook has the materials but doesn't know what to cook or how to plan a menu for the trek.

The cook can't cook: then sack him. Often within the service crew there will be someone who started as a cook, or has been a kitchen boy long enough and is ready for promotion. There are many things that can be taught to someone during the duration of a trek - basic cooking skills are not, usually, one of them. If the cook is really bad and has to go, then the WTL and the Sirdar will have to work this out amongst themselves and be very tactful and sensitive and hopefully have a demotion, rather than a redundancy. Remember there are only a few countries in the world that have any unemployment benefits and for a WTL to completely dismiss anyone - whether a Sirdar, cook or porter - can

What price a
hot shower?
Deforestation,
Nepal

seriously damage their re-employment prospects.

The cook isn't producing the goods because he doesn't have the raw materials. Whose fault is that, then? Well if the cook hasn't got them it's either because the Agent or Sirdar hasn't given him the goods, or the money to buy them, or the cook's pocketing the money or goods. Either way, it's you (the WTL) who has to sort it out, and do it quickly - ten days into the trek is too late, the rot has set in and you are probably too far away from civilisation to restock, whilst the cook/Sirdar/Agent has gambled away all of the money.

If the cook has the raw materials and isn't producing the goods then it's time to intervene again. Two likely problems here. Either he doesn't know what the trekkers want (Can you imagine being brought up in a remote mountain village learning to cook and then going into the world and having to cook for a Japanese group on one trip, a British the next, and a group of Californian Buddhists after that? And then you are handed all this pre-packed food and you can't read or write.) Or the problem is inexperience, and the cure for that is careful direction, again via the Sirdar.

The cook-boys (girls)
Although predominantly male, these are the darlings of the trekking world - as assistants to the cook they are the real grafters in the crew. Often first up and last to bed, they help the cook to clean, prepare and serve the meals, collect and wash the cutlery and crockery, dispose of the garbage and even bring the trekkers tea in the morning.

Points to watch out for here are the boys letting standards of hygiene drop either through ignorance or because they are in a hurry. The other danger they present is that they reinforce a view women have sought to prove for a long time - that males are capable of all domestic chores!

The cook-boys are often apprentice cooks in reality, and despite the long hours of the job they are held in quite high respect within the crew, are only answerable to the cook, are better paid than the porters, and are not far below the Sirdar's Assistants status-wise.

On big expeditions the kitchen crew will have their own porters, who will not only carry all the kitchen equipment but often the cook and cook-boys' personal gear as well. These porters tend not to carry as big a load as their colleagues which allows the kitchen to move en mass at an obscene pace, allowing them to set up at lunch-time and be first into camp each evening.

If you want to enamour yourself to the service crew, and the cook and his assistants in particular, then offer them a day off at some point during the trek when trekkers can cook and clean up for themselves. They probably won't take you up on the offer, but it is one way of showing your gratitude and respect for them. Don't forget, they not only cook for you, but often half of the service crew too.

If you want to make a complete pest of yourself then gang around the cook-tent demanding cups of tea or bowls of hot washing water twenty minutes before supper is due. Alternatively complain that the rubbish pit is too shallow and drink tea whilst watching the boys dig a bigger one. Failing that, try starting every sentence with "When I was on trek last year, we had a really good cook...".

The Porters

I still have moral dilemmas about using my fellow man as a beast of burden; in reality the porter rarely questions this. This is because the majority of porters are professional carriers, a profession that is centuries old, and one which has witnessed a recent revival due to the upsurge in trekking, with a general improvement in wages and conditions.

It still doesn't detract from the fact that someone else is carrying my bag. However, trekkers do, as a rule, pay more than the locals for porter services and ask them to carry less. This, combined with the equipment they are issued with and the end of trek tips, make portering on trekking expeditions the Third World equivalent of working on the oil-rigs. Porters work in different ways throughout the world. For years they had a notorious reputation for grinding expeditions to a halt by going on strike at the most inconvenient times. Strikes are not so common these days - in most countries where portering is common, their governments have laid down minimum wages and conditions and Sirdars, liaison officers and porters are well aware of these. I have witnessed Sirdars in several countries retain porters' ID cards, not only to ensure the right name goes on to the insurance document but also to ensure that the porters stick by the deal and work the length of the contract. Unfortunately, the porter doesn't usually have reciprocal rights forcing the Sirdar to keep to his word.

How much a porter carries varies, but most of the trekking companies will ask their porters to carry around 30kg, dropping to as little as 12kg at altitude, above the snowline or on nasty ground. Most porters are hired for a stage rather than by the day, the common routes having been broken down into stages years ago. So if you are hiring for yourself, check out if you are paying for a porter's services for the day or the stage - it is possible that a day's walk can cover several stages, which is quite a difference in price! Avoid the trek becoming an unending argument about finance and agree an all-inclusive price before setting out. This price should include a sum to cover for food and shelter, for returning home at the end of the trek, transport costs and equipment hire (as necessary) and payment during rest days.

Return payments occur when a trek finishes at a different point from the start, and the boys have to get back home, or when many porters are required. Think about the logistics involved and you'll soon realise that of 100 porters hired, 10 or 20 will be carrying food for porters, and that these 100 porters are eating a porter-load of food each or every other day. So as the expedition continues, the collective load it carries gets smaller daily and porters are sent back each day, usually being paid half-rates as compensation, particularly if there is no other work for them to bid for. The same rates apply for rest days, but these are commonly overlooked aspects of having a porter or porters, and ones that can prove to be very expensive when the big payout comes.

On big trips porters will ask for an advance on their wages, to allow them to stock up on food (and tobacco!) for the trip. If you have a Sirdar he will be doing the hiring and firing anyway, so refer these requests to him. If hiring yourself you cannot refuse this; just make sure your porter leaves his bed, including his possessions, with you whilst he goes off shopping. Many rucksacks have been seen for the last time disappearing into the bazaar, with the cry of "back in ten minutes, Sahib" landing in the dust of the porter's heels....

How much do you pay? Rates vary country to country, region to region and you really have to ask about the current prices. Local inflation will occur if a large Japanese expedition is in town, and often porters come cheaper by the dozen. One porter travelling with two trekkers will miss out on a great deal socially, something you must expect to pay for.

A small point to ponder: on an average 21 day commercial trek, porters outnumber trekkers by 2.5 to 1, eg. a group of ten, plus two leaders will probably have between 25-30 porters, plus Sirdar, cook, three cook-boys and three Sirdar's Assistants - a total of 48-55 people, and yet it works, because the porters seem to have the ability to blend into the landscape of camp.

The porters are the unsung heroes of the trekking scene, and often miss out on so many of the perks of the job. Without meaning to sound patronising these are the guys to get to know if you want to find out how a country is at grass-roots level, what a dollar is worth in the community, and how we are viewed as tourists. If you want to know how to milk a yak, light a fire with wet wood, operate an abacus or make sandals out of an old tyre you know who to ask.

Don't ever view your porter as a mule or you are doomed. They are human beings and as such will cheat, get drunk, fornicate and spit, carry your bag for a pittance, smile in the pouring rain, save every sweet you give them for their children and show concern for YOU, while you were having a bad day....

TOM'S STORY
Here is a story from another Tom, my father in this case, recalling the emotional impact of an incident in Pakistan.

"The eldest of our Balti porters, Sher Ali, came to our mess tent one evening with a nasty gash on his head. We cleaned it up and by using dumb-bell sutures managed to close the wound. After explaining to him that he must visit us every evening to have a clean dressing, he frowned slightly in acknowledgement and went off to join his companions.

Two days later we arrived at the edge of the Gondora glacier. The path had been swept away by a massive landslide caused by the spring melt, forcing us through the collapsing moraine and trying to avoid the many deep holes of ice water left by the glacier. With the continuing bombardment of falling boulders and moving earth, we were forced to run the gauntlet at a breathtaking pace to get through what we later called 'Hell-fire Pass'. It was a nightmare experience which left us shattered. To get out of danger we were presented with a 100ft snow gully to climb.

All the porters had already got to the top and were standing in a group waiting for us. I managed to climb about 20ft before I sank to my knees, exhausted, shaking like a leaf and gasping for breath.

Sher Ali knew my predicament, dropped his load and came running down the mountain slope, and taking my sack slowly helped me to the top of the gully and insisted on carrying my sack with his own load the remaining mile to the campsite.

Gasping my thanks, he smiled slightly, bowed and pointed to his head wound. Here was a man who, in his own way, had shown his appreciation for what we had done for him by his concern for my welfare and safety.

It made me feel so humble that thinking of it even now, many years later, brings a tear to my eye and a lump to my throat."

Tom Gilchrist

THE TREKKER - RESPONSIBILITIES
Whether you are on trek with just a couple of friends or as a member of a large group, individuals have certain obligations to the other members of the trek, the service crew and the WTL. First of all, let people get on with their job. If you want to take a more active part in running and operating the trek then do so

through the WTL, who will probably be very glad of your help but will also be very put out if you start digging loo pits or sorting out food without prior consultation. To start interfering with the service crew will cause confusion and discontent: consult your WTL before becoming involved.

Let your complaints be known. WTLs may be super-human but most cannot read minds. If you have a complaint then tell your leader and sort it out. Moaning to other trekkers will only serve to upset them and plant the seeds of discontent amongst the group. After a while you will be viewed as a moaner and your company avoided.

Before making that complaint ask yourself if it is really a genuine grievance, or a manifestation of your tiredness, anxiety or illness? Often a good fun day or a decent night's sleep can make so much difference, and the black view of eight hours earlier often pales to light grey. It's those old mental gymnastics.

Most illnesses and injuries can be sorted out pretty quickly if they are nipped in the bud - just tell the WTL as and when they occur. The alternative is to live with your conscience when you cross-infect the rest of the group or to watch from the sick tent as the rest of the party gain the summit.

Be punctual, especially in the morning. The camp can only be moved as soon as the last trekker has packed, eaten and walked off. Under most circumstances you can walk as slowly as you like during the day, but don't be the one holding everything up in camp. It is also a sure fire way to anger your fellow trekkers - they would have loved a long lie too, but felt obliged to the rest of the party....

Think and consider. Before draining the last of the soup - has everyone eaten? Before smoking indoors, before photographing, before opening your mouth....

How to annoy your WTL - advice to trekkers

1.   Be late.
2.   Ask them what their "real" job is.
3.   Ask them if they miss their girl/boyfriend, chocolate Hob Nobs/going down the pub/theatre.
4.   Ask them if they make a lot of money.
5.   Start every sentence with "It says in the brochure".
6.   Start every sentence with "When I was on trek last year, the leader did this...did that".
7.   Become annoyed when they don't know the name of every obscure peak.
8.   Become annoyed when they don't know the meaning of the name of every obscure peak.
9.   Wake them at 3am and ask for nail clippers, the correct time or a chocolate bar.
10. Tell them they drink too much tea.

11. Tell them that they don't deserve a day off because they are on holiday all the time....
12. Slurp your soup.
13. Snore!

Tipping

Tipping at the end of a trek is a bit more complicated than throwing some coins into a plate after a pleasant meal. If you don't approve of tipping, and refuse to tip at any time, then don't go on trek, because around the world the service crews see end of trek tips as part of their wage, and many would have turned down the work if they had known they weren't to be tipped at the end....

As the service crew is a tiny federal monarchy, workers are tipped according to their status rather than for their efforts. Thus the Sirdar scores considerably more than the porters, and we know who does most work...there is a widely used formula for working out who gets what.

Taking the porter as a base unit, tip him one day's wages for every week, or part week that he has worked for you. So in a 20 day trek he will receive an extra three days' wages (15%).

Next, give the kitchen boys 1.5 times this, ie. 4.5 days' porter wages.

Sirdar's assistants get twice the unit, ie. 6 days' porter wages. The cook three or four times, ie. 9 or 12 days' porter wages. And the Sirdar 5 or so days, ie. 15 days' porter wages. It's not a fair system but to tip someone above their station will create hell for them from above.... Sirdars are powerful guys and can make work very hard to get for those they don't like. Ditto cooks, cook-boys etc. So play the game, and don't rock the boat. Openly at least. There is no problem discretely tipping those you feel deserve it most, either with cash or with goods - unwanted clothes (particularly thermals, shirts etc.), head torches etc. Give away something of real value but of limited use, like an ice-axe or crampons, and you can expect them to be sold before you get back to the hotel...and why not? As WTL I always personally supervise giving away the tips. I didn't always and was horrified to discover one Sirdar who pocketed the lot for himself. He would probably have got away with it had he only kept two-thirds or half.

When giving a personal tip be very careful about not over-tipping, as this again can create problems from all levels. It's hard to be a discreet porter when someone tips you one or two weeks' extra wages. If you are not sure which porter was carrying your personal luggage during the trip, don't worry - during the last days of the trip you may find your bag personally collected and delivered too and from your tent by a smiling jovial character who looks vaguely similar to the miserable basket carrier, who, for two weeks, gave your kit bag a daily mud-bath and had it foot massaged by a rogue bull elephant.

Often an embarrassing show is made of giving out the tips, the only good thing being that at least everyone is together and you can get a good group photo, and it breaks up into a party afterwards. It's usually the service crew who want this, so go along with it - it's not a lot to ask after all they've done for you.

Many service crew members carry note books, and may ask you to write a reference for them. Some are very proud of these, and contain the signatures of some great contemporary mountaineers. Even if the crew don't understand what has been written because it is in English or German. It must have given J. Wright of Austin, Texas, great satisfaction when he wrote in one Sirdar's book:

"This man was a thorn in my side for ten days - if there is no one else in town to hire then wait until there is..."

It can work two ways.

Tipping the WTL is acceptable, indeed recommended by US trekking companies, as long as it is something small, and valuable. I promise I won't make a fuss.

THE TREKKER - ATTITUDES

"If our generation exploits everything available - the trees, the water or the minerals - without any care for the coming generations and the future then we are at fault, aren't we? But if we have a genuine sense of universal responsibility as our central motivation then our relating with the environment will be balanced, and so will our relations with our neighbours, both domestic and international".

His Holiness, the 14th Dalai Lama, Tenzin Gyatso: My Tibet

Camp toileting and garbage disposal signify more than just an organised camp - they represent a responsible attitude not only to the land but to the people who live on it. Using earth toilets and garbage pits requires discipline and for many of us this doesn't come easy and the rewards aren't that obvious to us, but they will be to other trekkers in years to come: when the land remains unspoiled and the locals smile and trekkers are still viewed as friends, even if our customs, language and motives remain enigmas.

If only it was that simple, that our responsibilities extended only to loos and rubbish, but the discipline needed in camp has to extend to our social behaviour if trekking, as we know it, is to continue. Trekking changes cultures, ways of life and people themselves, but only for the best if trekkers are responsible and consider other people.

Language

I'm not going to advocate that each trekker speaks fluent Trekland before going off on trek, but the more you can communicate verbally out in the wilds the more credibility and respect you'll earn. If you are not a linguist, then it is only polite to be able to thank your host, say "good morning" or "sorry" in his or her native tongue.

Photography

I'll reiterate a little on what was said in the last section - poking unwanted cameras into people's lives is not on, and in 99% of cases unnecessary, as most people are very happy to be photographed given ten minutes in your company as an introduction, and discreet portraits will not offend. Standing in the middle of a crowd with a 55mm lens is not discreet - paying locals and their children for photographs is strictly taboo.

Beggars

By giving to beggars, you create beggars. In most parts of the world true down and outs have to compete with acting down and outs for your coppers, and the more given, the more gaps appear in the marketplace, gaps created by well meaning folk. Even more insidious is that these beggars are often at the mercy of thugs who menace them for quite hefty cuts of their takings. And if that doesn't appeal to you then what about the parents who deliberately blind their children to make them more pitiful, purely so you'll dig deeper into your pocket....

By giving one sweet for one photograph you take away that first little piece of dignity and plant the seed that marks us as suckers and the posers as prostitues.

If you really want to help them there are ways. Giving cash to local charities is the easiest - usually run by locals who recognize the genuine needy from the impostors. International charities like Save the Children or Intermediate Technology, whose proven commitment to putting as much of our donations as possible into the field and not their administration or local gangsters, are accessible to us all via our local high street.

And if you want to give something to those gorgeous local children for giving you your best photo ever, how about ten minutes of your time - show them a photo of your children, your house, pull a face or do a conjuring trick. So they might view us as clowns...does it matter? Besides, have you ever seen a crowd of doe-eyed children turn nasty when the sweets run out? I'd rather run through a train full of Millwall supporters wearing a Chelsea scarf....

Souvenirs

Souvenirs? Hell's teeth, Gilchrist really is on a self-righteous kick! Well not really. I know you're really decent folk who wouldn't dream of doing this, but there are those who think it's okay to nose into people's houses and offer the householder, or in their absence the children, minute amounts for family heirlooms, carpets, musical instruments, jewellery, you name it. Others buy these things, but do it in the local market - just as you would at home.

A word about haggling. Some people are very good at haggling, some of us have "sucker" on our foreheads. By not haggling we raise the price for the next person coming along. Don't forget, because a trader *is* willing to haggle means his asking price is too high, even if it seems like a bargain to you. There is a principle at stake here! The best way to survive a price haggle is to price in your mind what you think the object is worth. Haggle to that price, try a bit lower, and if not settle at your level. If the trader agrees then you are more or less obliged to buy. Don't try laughing and saying "I was only practising my haggling..." If you do, then don't try whistling in the morning. Never reveal your true final price, because a good trader will always squeeze a little bit more out of you. Never show how desperately keen you are to have that Buddha carved out of coal, or you'll pay, pay, pay. I could go on - haggling is an art and can be good fun. It becomes tiresome, though, when you have to haggle for the same things, from the same man, every time you go on trek.

Food and fuel are usually a fixed price - ask around if you are not sure. The bit that stings most is when returning to camp, or the hotel, to find that your coal Buddha, very rare, seems to be one of the last two thousand in town. Except that yours is different - it costs twice as much as everyone else's. Smile, because most of the others have lied about the price, as a cover for the fact that they are rotten hagglers, and because the difference in price is buttons to you but the food bill for a family of four that day. Okay?

Ivory and furs and other wild animal products
The reasons for not buying wild animal products are, first, that they are illegal, second, that stocks are low, and likely to get so low as not to recover. Extinction, it's called. Buying one small piece of ivory leaves a space on someone's shop shelf that requires an elephant to die to allow restocking. This leaves an unfillable space for ever. Traders only exist because of consumer demand. Elephant stocks would start to recover if that demand stopped. I would have a public gallows at Elephantland International Airport where those caught with ivory products were publicly hanged beside the trader who sold them. "It hasn't worked with drugs!" I hear the crowd shout. True, but people don't get addicted to ivory, and it should slow the slaughter down enough to reverse the trend. Replace elephant with whale, tiger or whatever you choose - and sadly that choice is too large. I'll stop now - I'm getting dizzy up here on this soap box.

Drugs (narcotics)
If somebody knows of a country in the world where drugs are legal, I would be interested to know, because as far as I am aware they are illegal across every border. Which means that using recreational drugs leaves you at the mercy of the host country's laws, and courts, should you be caught. Being part of a group can implicate the others in your party - subjecting them to humiliating questioning and searches, and even seeing them convicted as accomplices. So, do not become involved with recreational drugs on trek because they are illegal and if caught, you could be fined, jailed or even executed.

Blending in, the author buying the latest fashion

Some countries in Asia and South America have a social approach to narcotics that directly contradicts that of their governments. The explanation is simple - governments take an official stand against narcotics so that they qualify for US and European favour and that means aid. However, no matter how lax the laws are at a local level, we as visitors are more open to prosecution because of the need to make an open international stand, to keep the sponsors happy.

There is sometimes pressure from locals to indulge in drugs, often at an almost innocuous level, as a cultural and social thing...but can you guarantee the dose, the strength of your sociable hit? Will you be able to keep trekking? A polite refusal very rarely causes offence. Best not to get involved, over-reactive as it may seem.

We as visitors are also susceptible to corruption at a local level. Our bribes are more than can be extracted from locals, and we do stand out. There are supposedly countries which run systems whereby informants earn a commission on the amount the guilty person is fined. The informant is often the dealer - if it's true you can't win, so why bother for the sake of a quick buzz?

Market day, Kashgar, China

Why take the risk if you don't know if it's rumour or not?

Drink
In Islamic countries the consumption of alcohol by Muslims is forbidden by law, and as in the case of drugs, implementation varies from not at all to national paranoia, and a blanket prohibition, regardless of whether one is a Muslim or not. As with drugs, we as visitors are bound by the laws of the land. Breaking the law leaves you open to prosecution if caught. Don't do it.

In other circumstances drinking too much leaves you open to nagging or upsetting others. It happens but try to avoid it.

Beware of local brews - seemingly innocuous, they are often strong enough to drop a horse. Brewing conditions are usually far from hygienic, with the process sometimes finishing in one's intestines - make sure your paper and lighter are close to hand!

Drink is dangerous at altitude and in the cold. As a stimulant it raises the heart-rate, which is fast enough already up high, and it effectively lowers the core temperature, which is not advisable. A wee dram does reduce stress though...just a wee one you understand....

Arguably the worst bit about drink on trek is the morning after - trying to get people going and forcing breakfast (fuel) inside them. And, of course, what are we trying to avoid daily on trek? Dehydration. What happens if you drink too much? You dehydrate...I'll stop there.

Dress

Coming from a society where the dress code is very relaxed it's hard to imagine, and easy to overlook, how the way we dress can cause offence. We are used to clothes that cling, and clothes that expose flesh. Bare arms, ankles and even heads that wouldn't cause a second glance at home could trigger a reaction in Trekland ranging from disgusted looks to being spat upon, stared at, or worse.

Physical reaction like those certainly increase one's level of awareness, though quiet disapproval, whilst being less obvious, is not necessarily an indication of a lesser degree of offence, or indignation felt. On the contrary, no reaction can be a greater measure of the offended's sensitivity, shock and disgust than our dress being so out-of-line that our standing is reduced to that of us being ignored.

If there is a tinge of sadness in these words then it's due to my melancholic reminiscence of witnessing the meeting of intelligent, friendly people, with the potential for lively intercourse, blocked because of discrepancies in cultural dress codes - a head-on thump of bigots. The trekker: 'Is it not time these people came into the 20th Century? This is how we dress, our culture'. The Local: 'How dare these people show their pinkie in front of my wife's sister? Of course I didn't tell them the rules, they should know them.'

There are a thousand absurdities on trek, dress being only twenty of them. Resign yourself to having the losing hand, find out the local dress taboos and heed them. Why? Because instead of being chastised you'll be rewarded - by being viewed with a more open mind and possibly, dare I say it, even liked. And that can't be bad.

Religious considerations

For the last century or so Britain, being a civilized country, has promoted religious tolerance amongst its citizens. The proliferation of places of worship and the diversity of religions and their breakaway sects bears testimony to this. Yet as a nation we are way down on the list of those countries that can be considered "religious". Few of us now consider the church as our prime source of guidance and comfort, yet throughout the third and developing worlds religion is important to the point of being the axis of the wheels of the nations' lives. Regardless of one's own views, religious commitment to this degree has to be respected, and to insult these religions is to personally insult the people themselves.

There is an arrogance amongst us poorly educated Westerners, promoted by the media, that gently mocks religions outwith our prevalent Christian/ Hebrew sects. The extremes of other religions are presented as their norms and the outrageous minority offered as the normal majority.

Rarely shown are the anomalies and absurdities of our own religions or the real effects that religion has on the majority of the world population. If, as Marx claimed "religion is the opium of the masses", then that drug is an anaesthetic helping alleviate some of the pain of poverty, a stimulant creating order out of the chaos of life, a sedative softening the blows of the harsh realities of life and death. Purpose, a reason for being, have come through clearly out of this opium haze for many, and what right have we to condemn or criticize because it makes others happy? Others have religion as we have departments of Health, Security, Employment and Social Work, providing all the financial and material benefits that ours offer.

There are counter - arguments, and as an evangelical atheist, I know them well, but these should be confined to home if religion in Trekland is of such importance to so many. We are trying to treat others as we like to be treated, so let's not go treading on others' religious toes. I've put in a little bit here about Buddhism, Islam and Hinduism not because these are the most important religions in the world, but because they are the most prominent in Trekland - and the most misunderstood.

Buddhism

The inner workings of Buddhism, like all religions, are complex, but are based on the belief that being open minded brings inner peace and that enlightenment comes through meditation. About 500 years older than Christianity, Buddhism is based on the teachings of its founder, Buddha, who defined the Four Noble Truths:

i)   Suffering is part of life.
ii)   Suffering is caused by selfishness.
iii)   Suffering will end if selfishness is destroyed by following
       the Eightfold Path. This is:
iv)   Understanding
       Thinking Clearly
       True Speech
       True Action
       Work
       Effort
       Mindfulness
       Contemplation.

The path leads to the state of Nirvana, attained once one is free from desire, hatred and ignorance. Until Nirvana is attained one is caught in the cycle of birth, death and rebirth. Prayers are made not to God, but to the Buddha within and take the form of meditation.

As a worldwide religion with over 200 million followers, the highest concentration being in Asia, it is only natural that Buddhism has evolved in many different forms. As Buddhism teaches that there is no soul, many of the ceremonial rites of passage - birth, death and the onset of puberty - are marked by ceremonies "borrowed" from the host or other cultures, so on the periphery Buddhism can appear to take many forms.

Most trekkers first encounter Buddhism in Nepal, despite it being a minority religion there. It has a high profile due to the large numbers of Tibetan refugees, and because of its prominence in the high, and popular, valleys of the Everest region where the local tribe, the Sherpas, are Buddhist. It is also common in Ladakh, another popular Trekland.

Festivals are many and follow common themes - the demarcation of the seasons, breaks in the work pattern, etc. To avoid offence bear in mind these common Buddhist vows:

Do not harm any living thing.	Do not speak wrongly.
Do not take what is not given.	Do not use drugs or drink alcohol.
Do not mis-use your senses.	

Also be aware that fires are considered sacred, so always ask before adding anything to the flames. You must also pass prayer stones and prayer wheels to your right side. Always ask for permission before entering temples or attending religious ceremonies.

Hinduism

Hinduism is a very ancient religion probably dating back to about 2500BC. Ironically, it originated in the Indus valley of what is now Pakistan. A complex religion, it has been around longer than most, thus allowing it to become extremely diverse, though sharing the same common themes - there is only one god, Brahman, and that the soul is reincarnated until salvation (Moshka) is attained. Hindus have great respect for all living things and the family and follow Dharma, a strict code of honesty, justice, self-control, charity and religious tolerance. They differ in belief from Buddhists in that in attaining Moshka, the soul is reunited with God, as opposed to gaining perfect and lasting peace through enlightenment.

The tight structure of Hinduism created the caste system, resulting in what, to non-Hindus at least, is an appalling social class system. At the top are the Brahmans (priests and brains), then come the Kshatriyas (warriors and rulers), followed by the Vaisayas (traders and farmers) and then the poor old Sundras (artisans and lower orders). Society being as it is, each caste also has its own sub-castes, leaving lower order Sundras in a pretty wretched state socially and politically.

Worship tends to be on a self-governing, individual basis, with large congregations usually only on special occasions, eg. weddings or festivals. The apparent multitude of gods worshipped are, in fact, representations of the many facets of the One. Graphic representation is one of the characteristics of Hinduism, often being central to worship.

For trekkers, offence is most likely to be created by blaspheming and by not

Sub-Alpine:
Monte Rotondo,
Corsica

observing the holiness of cows - especially in India. It is worth removing labels from such food products as dried milk, corned beef (and at least one cheese spread) if you are taking food into a Hindu country.

Islam
Muslims believe in one God, Allah, and model their lives on the teachings of Allah as written down in their holy book, the Qur'an. This was revealed by Allah to his prophet, Mohammed, who was born in Mecca in AD570. Mohammed stated that the religion of Islam is supported by Five Pillars. They are Shahada: the confession of faith; Salat: prayer (five times daily); Sawm: fasting; Zakat: charity; and Hajj: pilgrimage.

To a muslim, his prayer mat is his own place of worship, but when possible prayers are made in the mosque - sometimes a plain affair, often ornate but never containing any representations of Allah or his prophet. Shoes must be removed before entering the mosque and prayers are preceeded by Wazu - ritual ablutions.

Women pray separately from the men, and both sexes wear decent and moderate clothing at all times, covering the face, legs and arms. Others are expected to do the same. The head is usually covered during prayer - prayers being made facing the holy city of Mecca.

Muslims believe that God sent prophets to teach his people, Jesus being one of them. He is not considered divine, as Christians believe him to be, and this has become a bone of contention for generations, sadly inhibiting mutual

Ishkamin Valley, Pakistan

respect between the two religions.

Festivals are frequent in the Islamic calendar and are commemorations of Allah's revelations to Mohammed or mark significant moments in the prophet's life.

Whilst seemingly a harsh religion, Islam promotes not only the equality of all men, but also that all living things are the creation of Allah and as such must be treated with care and kindness. Muslims are forbidden to eat pork, and any meat eaten must have come from animals that have been ritually killed. Alcohol is also forbidden. Physical displays of affection are frowned upon and women are discouraged from "revealing their beauty to others". How easy it is to offend is very dependent on the general attitude of the country concerned. The sight of a non-muslim drinking beer in a pavement cafe wouldn't raise an eyebrow in Morocco but would lead to an arrest in Saudi Arabia. Scant clothing will cause offence though - even when worn by men. Islam is a way of life, remember, as well as a religion. As pictorial representations are very uncommon, strict Muslims will take offence at being photographed, as will women.

Finally, as ablutions are performed using the left hand, eat only with the right hand...but don't worry if you are left-handed - indicate this and allowances will be made.

Evangelism
If you want to become a missionary then see your spiritual leader. Being on trek is a totally inappropriate situation to try and convert either the locals or your fellow trekkers. Inconsiderate born-again Christians on trek are justification for born-again lions. Religious tolerance is the name of the game.

CHAPTER EIGHT

Theft, loss and other emergencies

THEFT / LOSS

On realising a theft don't give in to that soul sapping, gut churning, lethargy inducing depression. Have a good cry, a bit of a worry, and try and find your stuff! Ask around and look about you. Rural communities can be acutely embarrassed by the prospect of having a thief amongst their midst and are able to exert considerable underground pressure on the culprits. Certainly if nothing is said, the chances of stolen property turning up will be slim. Tell the police - even the illiterate village bobby - and don't underestimate their power, influence or local knowledge. Tell other trekkers - the thieves may try to sell your stuff on...just let it be known, if nothing else, to warn others!

If all your funds, your passport and even your plane ticket home have been lost or stolen then take comfort in the fact that at least you are insured. I know you are insured because the kind of person who travels uninsured doesn't read information like this: instead, they end up stuck out on a limb, hassling their Embassy for help and begging off tourists. Having a phone number to ring for help is very comforting and your insurers will give you a 24 hour contact number should the worst happen.

Passport

The only people who can renew, replace or extend your passport in Trekland are members of the diplomatic staff in the British Embassy. They are not going to replace your passport unless they are convinced that you and your loss are genuine. This may involve them making a few enquiries, which may take a little time: having a photocopy of your documents may help move things along. In the meantime they should be able to help you with the necessary phone calls and also to arrange for funds to be transferred from home to Trekland. Sometimes they may even give you a minor loan or act as guarantors to allow you to run up credit in hotels and restaurants - but rarely with a smile, and don't look for any sympathy. Apart from the passport side of things, your agent is a better bet as he will know local hotels for you to stay in on tick, know which police officers to talk to concerning your loss or theft, and hopefully be able to sort out a statement from them for your insurers. He will also have a bank account to transfer funds to - much easier and quicker than having to collect at a bank. Especially if you have no passport. Banks are notoriously inefficient at transferring funds, ie. those in Trekland. It helps if you can use an international bank like Grindley's or American Express.

If you've had credit cards or travellers cheques stolen, inform the issuing body immediately so that they can prevent them being used further and arrange for replacements as soon as possible.

Plane tickets will be replaced as long as you know your flight details, ie. whom you are flying with, and the date and time you are meant to be flying. This is such a rare occurrence that it is unlikely there will be any hassle or extra charges, but do inform the airline of your loss as soon as possible.

RESCUE

Pre-departure

Whilst prevention is obviously better than cure, being in an extremely unpredictable environment (the outdoors) with an unpredictable product (human beings), even the most cautious trekkers can only REDUCE the odds of an accident happening. So be prepared for the worst and hope it doesn't happen.

How is your first-aid? Being part of a trek, regardless of whether you are a paying client or a trek leader, you should have a knowledge of first-aid that extends to you holding a first-aid certificate. It is irresponsible to presume that someone else is going to handle "that side of things". And remember, holding a first-aid certificate only means you were deemed competent on the day you passed that exam - constant revision is necessary to maintain that level of skill and to keep abreast of new developments.

Before departing on trek some potential bureaucratic problems can be anticipated, and hopefully avoided with a little preparation. This involves listing all your known medical allergies and medical conditions. Your date of birth, address, passport number, expiry date, visa number, flight number, insurer's name, emergency phone number and a copy of your insurance cover-note. Put all this information on one sheet and attach a passport photo. Leave one copy with your agent (if you are using one), another with the British Embassy and keep one yourself, or preferably with your leader or in the first-aid/medical box. Make sure each page has a photo attached. One of yourself.

A word about helicopters. They are expensive to run, despite being, in most cases, little bigger than a car. Most operators will not turn a rotor until they know who is going to be paying for their services. And in most cases we're talking cash up front. Most trekkers don't have that cash. They need a guarantee that you'll pay up a bond. A good agent will provide this or try the Embassy - you'll need to show them your insurance documents before they'll open the door for you.

Now, if you have to order a helicopter, there should be three sources who can tell the operators what they want to know - who is going to pay, who is going to secure that payment, and whom they are going to pick up. It also means that if evacuation outwith the country is necessary then the agent can go ahead and arrange a visa (if necessary), and the Embassy can either arrange clearance with the Civil Aviation Authority for an air ambulance or can start proceedings with airlines and prime the emergency services about the patient they are about to receive.

Whilst someone is diving around dropping this information off, another can be collecting information on where the nearest radio stations are on your trekking route and marking them on the map.

And before you go trekking - is that first-aid kit/medical box as it should be?

On trek

If the worst should happen, and there has been an accident, the first thing is to STAY CALM. A headless chicken will help no-one. Except in a few instances, a two minute reflection on the situation and your own state of mind is an investment in time that will pay enormous dividends as events develop. Stand back for a minute or two, calm down, and get the whole thing in perspective.

There are three considerations: the casualty, the other trekkers and the support crew.

The casualty. Is the casualty in a stable, safe position, healthwise and environmentally? If not then ensuring they are is a priority.

The other trekkers. Are they safe? Is everyone calm and coping with the situation? Consider appointing a leader to keep everything in order. The trauma of witnessing an accident can often induce hysteria or shock in a third party. Keep everyone together though, because their labour may be required later on.

The support crew. Stop the circus! Send a racing porter to the front of the procession and stop the whole show. It's a good excuse for a brew, so try and get a cook-boy back to the scene of the incident. Hot, sweet tea can often surpass any medical alternative. If it's a minor accident, then a half hour break will make little difference to the day. If it's more than minor, then knowing where the equipment and manpower is could save a life.

Stopping the expedition literally in its tracks is, like so much of this advice, only advice. The decision can only be made by you in that unique situation. Comfort and safety will dictate. Why stop everything five minutes from that day's camp? Why go on when you are only ten minutes from your last one? The answers lie in the severity of the accident.

Assessing the casualty's condition means going back to the first-aid. Let's presume the worst and that an evacuation is necessary. There are two alternatives: 1. The casualty is able to make an assisted retreat, ie. walking wounded. 2. The casualty needs a litter evacuation, either carried or flown out. 1. If the casualty can walk but cannot continue with the expedition, ie. broken collar bone, or a stabilised upper body injury, then either the trek splits and the fit continue but the casualty and a companion retreat, or everyone retreats. In most cases the former is the case. A mini service crew will have to be arranged to support them, of course - and don't forget any relevant paper work - trekking permits etc. Don't leave the injured person to cope with their retreat alone - apart from the comfort of having a companion, it is essential that someone else be there in the event of the casualty's condition deteriorating. 2. Should the injured person be unable to walk then we enter into the complexities of a stretcher evacuation. First of all you'll need two, possibly three things: a stretcher, a carrying crew and a helicopter.

The stretcher
Unless you are a hyper-organised, belt and braces outfit this will have to be an improvised affair. Ski-poles, ropes, Karrimats, flysheets, tent poles, green timber are all potential stretcher - building skills. (Something else to ponder over at home prior to going trekking.) Points to consider are: 1. The nature of the casualty's injury. 2. The duration of the carry - is the stretcher strong enough? Also, if someone is being stretchered, it is usually advisable not to move the casualty more than is necessary. So the stretcher could become their bed for a few days - make it as comfortable as possible. 3. Security - ensure the casualty doesn't fall off the stretcher or that their injuries are made worse by them being moved.

The power
It has been estimated that it takes three interchanging crew of eight people to carry a stretcher one mile in one hour - twenty-four people per hour. Professional porters in Trekland will do much better than this, but be prepared to have to pay bonuses and have to impress on them the fragility of their cargo. Make frequent stops to ensure the stretcher and the patient are as relaxed, secure and as comfortable as is possible under the circumstances.

Being on a stretcher can be very frightening and disorientating. Try and keep everyone as calm and quiet as possible, don't crowd round the casualty and offer as much reassurance as is possible and necessary. Sometimes, an alternative to being stretchered out is to be carried piggy-back. Best left to a professional carrier, this is quick, easy to arrange and requires less labour. Usually the carrier takes the casualty on his back with a trump line under the casualty's behind and round the carrier's head. The carrier will definitely need guidance, and help with the casualty when stopping and starting. The casualty's rump will need extra padding!

Most carries should be fairly short - to the nearest helicopter landing site, or road, unlike in the good old days.

Before going any further, a word about helicopters. They do not defy the laws of gravity but are still bound by them and fly by virtue of some basic physics and rudimentary mechanical principals. How high they fly depends on the density of the air in which their little rotors whirl round. In the mountains the density can vary enormously and whilst technically a helicopter can work at altitudes up to 6,100m, 5,000m is a more realistic ceiling and 4,500m a far safer alternative.

So bear altitude in mind when you start to think about helicopters and evacuations. But first find your chopper. As soon as you realise you need a helicopter find a messenger that speaks and reads English as well as his or her native tongue. Locate your nearest possible landing site. (You can never presume that the helicopter will have facilities to winch, so accept that they will need to land.) In practical terms we're talking about a level area 30m x 30m, clear of vegetation. Locate your nearest radio station.

Prepare a message to be transmitted. Keep it simple, in English and Trek tongue, and copy it three times. It must state: 1. Who the message is for - your agent or Ambassador. 2. Who the casualty is, their condition, DOB and passport number. 3. The location of the landing site - grid reference, map title and edition. Give a few aids to the location - the altitude, a nearby landmark, ie. the name of a village, pass or peak. Altitude is important, as previously mentioned, but also because it can seriously affect the chopper's fuel needs and its possible payload. 4. Any special needs, eg. oxygen, traction splint or doctor. There is no guarantee that any requests will be acknowledged - often the choppers are civilian craft and you'll be lucky if there's a stretcher on board or the crew have any medical training. Be very grateful if the chopper arrives at all, and when it does be prepared to remain in charge. 5. Who the message is from: your name and the company's name. KEEP THE MESSAGE CLEAR.

Send the message, wrapped in some kind of waterproof container, off to the radio post with your messenger. Send a pal with him and give him a copy too. Waterproofed. Give the prophets enough funds to 1. Possibly bribe the radio operators. 2. Feed themselves - they may be away for some days. 3. Return home if it proves impossible for them to be reinstated with the expedition.

Prepare to move the casualty to the landing site. Will there be enough time to manage this in one day? If not, does everyone have the necessary equipment to allow a bivi? Think it through.

Move the casualty to the evacuation site. It may be worth sending someone on ahead to clear the site in preparation and be there just on the off-chance that the helicopter arrives before the casualty. Whether the helicopter shuts down its engine or not (usually not) you pay for the time they are out. Mark the landing site if possible, with a tarpaulin or tent fly, and be prepared to remove it as the chopper approaches. I know, the down draft blows things away, but like a didgeridoo player, helicopters seem to be able to blow and suck at the same time, and a tarpaulin sucked into a rotor or air intake will down the craft. Do leave up some kind of secure windsock so the pilot is aware of the wind direction.

Ideally the casualty should be 50-100m away, sheltered from the down draft and the general mayhem of a machine that can hover.

Wait for the helicopter. Be prepared for a long wait - up to a week. So have suitable provisions with you. With the casualty should be 1. Written personal details (name, age, date of birth, passport number, trekking or climbing permit [if appropriate], contact address, ie. consul or agent, details of injury and medication given, pulse and temperature chart, any known allergies). This is just in case weight restrictions prevent the casualty being accompanied. 2. Personal bits and bobs, specs, false teeth, wallets etc. Those hoping to accompany the casualty should divide their baggage - a small day bag with toothbrush, clean knickers, wallet, passport, etc., with the remainder in as few bags as possible - again weight restrictions.

When the helicopter arrives - give a quick prayer of thanks then stay well out of the way until it lands. This will be into the wind if possible. Approach the craft from the front - the pilot usually sits on the same side as we drive on - and crouch down so the pilot can see you, and outwith the radius of the rotors - they have been known to dip almost to the ground on landing. (Tail rotors can hypnotise - soldiers on exercise have been killed by walking into them entranced.) When the pilot is ready he will signal you forward to his door.

Ensure there is nothing loose that could be drawn near the rotors or engines, eg. hats, scarves and general kit.

Load the chopper - remember the crew may not necessarily be medics or have brought your stretcher as requested. Stay in control and be assertive! If someone's hurt be sure the pilot will stay well out of it! And then fly off into the blue yonder, civilisation and the end of all your troubles. Possibly.

THIRD WORLD HOSPITALS

I never realised how much I'd taken our hospitals for granted until I had cause to use a hospital in Nepal - one of the better ones in Kathmandu, and the only one with beds available. I was with a friend, Dave, who had broken his femur, and it had taken us three days to get there. On arrival at reception payment had to be made up front for admission, x-rays and examination by a doctor. The x-ray was a trial. First we had to wait for electricity - there had been a power cut and the emergency generator was having problems. Then I had to help the x-ray technician move Dave onto the table and hold him there whilst he was photographed. Lead shields? What are they? After this it was up to the ward, a double room, the other occupant being a rather elderly gentleman with a badly fractured skull. Sadly, he died within a few hours and Dave had the room to himself. The other three beds were for attendant relatives - the hospital, as is normal in Asia, had no domestic staff or auxiliary nurses so all the work they normally do has to be done by the relatives - cleaning, feeding, bathing, changing. Meals were available at a small extra cost, but they were terrible and the timing spasmodic. I was expected to move into the hospital ward too and do all these things but I couldn't - I had to stay in a hotel so that

I could be near the phone and the fax to arrange Dave's repatriation. It was bedlam running back and forth with food and sheets from the hotel, washing Dave, emptying his bed-pan etc. Things got worse - Dave's fracture required some heavy-duty nuts and bolts surgery to put right and there was a six week waiting list for the surgeons. Delhi had the nearest available operating theatre so that's where he had to go - by private jet courtesy of his insurance company. Of course we didn't have visas for India, and would the Indians give us one in a hurry? Does Mother Theresa play rugby?

Eight days after Dave broke his leg he was operated on. Successfully, I must add, and it all ended happily. The moral of his story is to be aware that hospitals outside the first world are not always what you would expect nor the end of your troubles. Be prepared to be nurse, cleaner and cook. This was a good hospital that had many Europeans, who could speak English, as volunteers on the medical staff and who really took it upon themselves to look after Dave and at least gave him the best medical attention possible. Another friend of mine, a nurse, found himself in hospital in Pakistan having to show the nurses how to insert a drip into himself. He again was flown home and made a full recovery, courtesy of the insurers. Second moral to the story - make sure you are insured.

Both the stories I've mentioned happened in hospitals that were fairly well equipped. Not all are, hence all these bits and pieces of seemingly unnecessary medical equipment on the contents list of the recommended medical kit. And don't forget those receipts.

The very worst scenario
In the event of a death on trek the immediate problem is whether to repatriate the body or to bury or cremate there and then. In remote areas the former may prove to be impossible. Should this be the case and a burial or cremation is the only option, try where possible to have a third party give a written testimony about the death and subsequent interment, preferably a local doctor, statesman or policeman. Tasteless as it may seem, take photographic evidence. Then take all personal effects, and ashes if appropriate, to the nearest Embassy and ask them about death certificates and what to do next.

Repatriation is easy enough once you reach civilisation - airlines are familiar with what to do and will make all the arrangements for you. Reaching civilisation is the hard part. To many cultures, keeping a corpse above ground for more than a day is totally alien and offensive to them and finding porters may prove very hard. The only practical way of moving a body back to civilisation is by helicopter, but how realistic is that in view of the difficulties involved in getting a chopper in to airlift an injured person? Again with repatriation, contact the Embassy as soon as is possible. And that's all I'm going to say on this subject.

Tailpiece

When my dad was 63 years old we went on trek together for the first time. My dad does not take kindly to heat, dust, foreign food, altitude or strange beds. So we went trekking in Pakistan. Within the first three days he had been on a harrowing internal flight, spent a night in a Baltistani truck drivers' "hotel", and had been crammed into a bald-tyred jeep piloted by a complete psychopath for a sixteen hour drive up what can only be described as a ledge carved along the side of a crumbling mountain. We got out at 3,000 odd metres and camped in the shade of a poplar tree. It was 42°C. Things went not too badly for the next week or so until dad caught a tummy bug at 5,000m. My dad is cautious and considers new proposals very carefully. He also likes his comforts and privacy, and being a canny Scot views change with suspicion. He had taken a lot of persuasion to go to Pakistan. So what did we talk about in our tent at 5,000m? Everything, including planning our next trek together.

Many trekkers go trekking only once, but very few of them do so out of choice. I know many trekkers, who have been on many treks, whose first trek was a one off, chance in a lifetime, never to be repeated trip.... Which of course it was. As was the next one, and the one after that. Talk to them about their treks and you'll be regaled with desperate tales of illness, hardship and what didn't go according to plan. But read between the lines, or see behind that thousand yard stare, and you might just catch a glimpse of alpenglow, or the smell of wild flowers caught on a mountain breeze, feel the warmth of good companions. Listen carefully and maybe you'll hear that lullaby, sung in an unknown tongue, carry through the still night.

My mother told me about my father's trek. Because he talked about it a lot. Like a talking *National Geographic*, she said. She wrote and told me about the changes that a month away had made to this man she had known for forty-two years. Of how he had become more tolerant and less complaining. Of the sparkle of life in his eyes. Of how he had lost nearly a stone in weight.... I'll see you out there.

Printed in Great Britain by
St Edmundsbury Press Limited, Bury St Edmunds, Suffolk